The Illustrated History of
EARLY MAN

The Illustrated History of
EARLY MAN

John Haywood

SMITHMARK

This edition published in 1995
by SMITHMARK Publishers Inc.
16 East 32nd Street
New York, New York 10016.

SMITHMARK books are available for bulk
purchase for sales promotion and premium
use. For details write or telephone the
Manager of Special Sales, SMITHMARK
Publishers Inc., 16 East 32nd Street, New
York, NY 10016. (212) 532 6600.

Produced by Brompton Books Corp.,
15 Sherwood Place,
Greenwich, CT 06830

ISBN 0-8317-1754-8

Printed in Spain

10 9 8 7 6 5 4 3 2 1

Page 1: Cave painting of bison from Lascaux, France.
Upper Paleolithic *c.* 15,000 years old.

Page 2: Chimpanzee using a stick to dig for roots.
The chimpanzee's ability to use simple tools may
give clues to help us understand how our own
primate ancestors first learned how to use and make
tools.

These pages: The great upright stones of Stonehenge,
England, weigh over 50 tons each and were brought
to the site from 24 miles (38km) away. Such
monuments show what prehistoric societies could
achieve using only well organized muscle power and
simple levers. The main phase of the stone circle
was completed *c.* 2120 BC.

Contents

Introduction

From the earliest times, humans have sought to explain their origins through myth but the scientific study of early man dates only from the early nineteenth century. Calculations based on the Bible suggesting that the world had been created in 4004 BC, were overturned when the geologist Charles Lyell (1797-1875) demonstrated that the world was in fact many millions of years old, forcing antiquarians and historians to question their assumptions about the length of human history. Archeology also developed as a scientific discipline in this period as a result of the Danish antiquarian C. J. Thomsen's introduction, in 1819, of the "three age" system based on successive phases of technological development: the Stone Age, the Bronze Age, and the Iron Age. Though the Stone Age was later subdivided into Paleolithic (Old Stone Age), Mesolithic (Middle Stone Age), and Neolithic (New Stone Age), Thomsen's system still forms the basic framework for the study of human prehistory. However, the study of artifacts for their own sake is no longer central to modern archeology, which now seeks to use increasingly sophisticated techniques to reconstruct the social structures, economies, and environments of prehistoric communities. As a result our understanding of some of the major developments of human history, such as the adoption of farming and the origins of civilization, has been revolutionized in recent years.

The most important development in the study of early man, however, was the publication, in 1859, of Charles Darwin's *On the Origin of Species*. Though Darwin's thesis did not explicitly discuss human origins, its implications were clear enough. Man, like any other animal species, had evolved from a more primitive ancestor: he had not been specially created. Darwin's thesis outraged the conventionally religious, but his proposed mechanism of evolution, "the survival of the fittest," was very much in accord with the rugged individualism of nineteenth-century industrial civilization and it rapidly gained wide acceptance. However, mankind has proved reluctant to relinquish

Left: Coptic wall painting of Adam and Eve, sixth century AD, Cairo. According to the Book of Genesis, God fashioned Adam, the first man, out of dust and breathed in his nostrils to give him life. When Adam became lonely God removed one of his ribs while he slept and from it created Eve, the first woman, to be his companion. Only in the nineteenth century was the Biblical account of creation challenged.

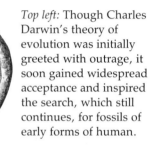

Top left: Though Charles Darwin's theory of evolution was initially greeted with outrage, it soon gained widespread acceptance and inspired the search, which still continues, for fossils of early forms of human.

Above and left: The recognition that human technology had developed through successive stages from simple stone tools to tools of easily worked metals like copper and bronze and finally iron, led to the introduction of the "three age" system of Stone, Bronze, and Iron Ages. This still forms the basic framework for the study of human prehistory. A finely worked stone spearhead, from Tennessee, after 10,000 BC (*bottom left*), a bronze sword, Bavaria, 1200-700 BC (*bottom right*), and an iron spearhead and plow share, India, first millennium BC (*top right*).

completely its special place in creation and research into human evolution has always been colored by our preconceptions of what we are. The most illuminating example of this is the famous case of Piltdown Man. To the technologically minded Victorians, it was plain that what separated humans from other animals was tool use. Our ape ancestors, they believed, had learned how to use simple tools and this was so advantageous that natural selection favored the evolution of greater intelligence to allow more effective tool use.

Anthropologists therefore expected our earliest ancestors to be large-brained apes. When bones apparently confirming this belief were found in a gravel pit at Piltdown in southern England in 1912, the scientific

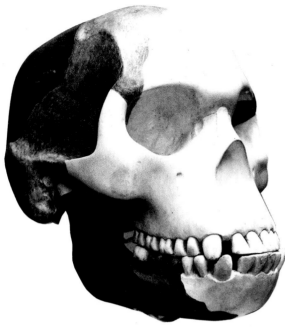

Left: Cast of a reconstruction of the skull of Piltdown Man. Piltdown Man was one of the most successful scientific hoaxes ever perpetrated. Hailed at first as the "missing link," the remains were eventually discovered to be a mixture of modern ape and human bones stained to make them look old.

Right: Egyptian scribes: the development of writing was of vital importance to the growth of civilization.

Timechart of Early Human History

Years Before Present: 5 million | 4 million | 3 million | 2 million | 1.5 million | 1 million | 750,000 | 500,000 | 250,000 | 100,000 | 50,000

Geological epochs: PLIOCENE | PLEISTOCENE ("ICE AGE")

Hominid species:
- *Australopithecus ramidus* (earliest hominid)
- *A. afarensis*
- *A. africanus*
- *A. robustus*
- *A. boisei*
- *Homo habilis*
- *Homo erectus*
- Archaic *Homo sapiens*
- *H. sapiens sapiens*
- *H. sapiens neanderthal[ensis]*

Africa:
- "Lucy"
- 3.6 million-year-old hominid footprints (Laetoli, Tanzania)
- Earliest tools (Hadar, Ethiopia)
- Earliest evidence of human use of fire (Chesowanya, Kenya, and Swartkrans, South Africa)
- Handaxes first manufactured
- *H. sapiens sapiens* migrates out of Africa into Near East
- Earliest musical instrument (flute, North Africa)

Europe:
- Earliest *H. erectus* in Europe ("Boxgrove Man," England)
- Possible earliest human structure (hut, Terra Amata, France)
- Oldest known wooden tool (spear, Clacton, England)
- *H. [sapiens] in [Europe]*

Asia:
- *H. erectus* finds in Java
- Earliest *H. erectus* finds in Near East
- *H. erectus* in China ("Peking Man")
- *H. sapiens sapiens* in Near East

Australia and Pacific:
- *H. sapiens sapiens* in Australia
- Voyages to Pac[ific] islands begin

The Americas:
- Settlemen[t] (15,000–12[...])

establishment was delighted and accepted their authenticity without question. Only in 1953 was it discovered that Piltdown Man was a fake, made up out of the cleverly disguised jaw of a modern orangutan and the cranium of a modern human, both of which had been stained with tea to make them look old.

Despite this embarrassing lesson, modern anthropologists remain less than perfectly objective in their approach as the continuing acrimonious debate between the adherents of the main rival theories of human evolution demonstrates all too clearly. The study of early man continues to be a volatile and fast-moving discipline: it is the purpose of this book to provide a clear and up-to-date introduction to this long and vitally important period of human history.

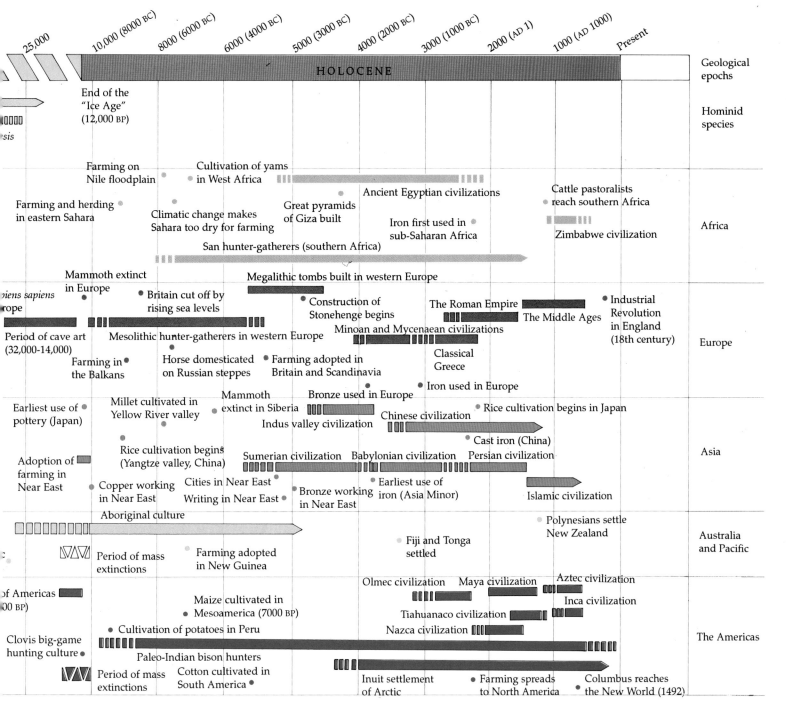

	25,000	10,000 (8000 BC)	8000 (6000 BC)	6000 (4000 BC)	5000 (3000 BC)	4000 (2000 BC)	3000 (1000 BC)	2000 (AD 1)	1000 (AD 1000)	Present	
					HOLOCENE						Geological epochs
	End of the "Ice Age" (12,000 BP)										Hominid species
	Farming on Nile floodplain	Cultivation of yams in West Africa				Ancient Egyptian civilizations		Cattle pastoralists reach southern Africa			
Farming and herding in eastern Sahara		Climatic change makes Sahara too dry for farming	Great pyramids of Giza built			Iron first used in sub-Saharan Africa		Zimbabwe civilization			Africa
			San hunter-gatherers (southern Africa)								

Mammoth extinct in Europe
Megalithic tombs built in western Europe
piens sapiens *rope*
Britain cut off by rising sea levels
Construction of Stonehenge begins
The Roman Empire
Industrial Revolution in England (18th century)
The Middle Ages
Period of cave art (32,000-14,000)
Mesolithic hunter-gatherers in western Europe
Minoan and Mycenaean civilizations
Classical Greece
Farming in the Balkans
Horse domesticated on Russian steppes
Farming adopted in Britain and Scandinavia
Europe

Mammoth Bronze used in Europe
Iron used in Europe
Earliest use of pottery (Japan)
Millet cultivated in Yellow River valley
extinct in Siberia
Rice cultivation begins in Japan
Chinese civilization
Indus valley civilization
Cast iron (China)
Rice cultivation begins (Yangtze valley, China)
Sumerian civilization Babylonian civilization Persian civilization
Adoption of farming in Near East
Copper working in Near East
Cities in Near East
Writing in Near East
Bronze working in Near East
Earliest use of iron (Asia Minor)
Islamic civilization
Asia

Aboriginal culture
Polynesians settle New Zealand
Period of mass extinctions
Farming adopted in New Guinea
Fiji and Tonga settled
Australia and Pacific

Olmec civilization Maya civilization Aztec civilization
of Americas *00 BP)*
Maize cultivated in Mesoamerica (7000 BP)
Inca civilization
Tiahuanaco civilization
Cultivation of potatoes in Peru
Nazca civilization
Clovis big-game hunting culture
Paleo-Indian bison hunters
The Americas
Period of mass extinctions
Cotton cultivated in South America
Inuit settlement of Arctic
Farming spreads to North America
Columbus reaches the New World (1492)

CHAPTER ONE

Before Man

The human species is unique. Other living organisms have adapted through evolution to suit the environments in which they live. Humans are physically adapted to live only in a tropical environment, yet because we have the ability to modify our surroundings to suit ourselves, we have colonized a greater part of the Earth than has any other species. By lighting fires, making clothing, and building shelters, our ancestors discovered how to survive and even flourish in climates in which a naked human would quickly perish. Through agriculture, engineering, and industry, modern humans have gone further and created entirely new environments – not all of them healthy – and have achieved, through our unrivaled ability to manipulate our surroundings, enormous influence over the future of life on this planet. Many humans now live in largely artificial environments with little direct contact with the natural world. Human behavior is, to a great extent, culturally determined and learned rather than instinctive, making it all too easy to imagine that we are not a part of nature. However, these unique aspects of human behavior are relatively recent developments, dating only from around 100,000-40,000 years ago: most of our ancestors would have appeared to us to be much more like animals than humans in their behavior.

Humans belong to the order of mammals known as primates, the order which includes the lemurs and lorises, the Old and New World monkeys, and our closest relatives, the apes: gibbons, orangutans, gorillas, and chimpanzees. Because of the

Right: The common ancestor of humans, gorillas, and chimpanzees evolved in a rainforest environment similar to this rainforest reserve in Nigeria.

Below: Orangutan crossing a river, Kalimantan, Indonesia. Of the apes, orangutans are the best adapted to an arboreal lifestyle and are not as closely related to humans as chimpanzees and gorillas. Orangutans are thought to descend from the ramapiths, a group of apes which flourished 12 million years ago.

physical similarities between them and humans, apes are classified as hominoid, that is, human-like. Like humans, apes are generally larger than other primates, have larger brains, fully opposable thumbs, and lack tails. Apes also suffer from many of the same diseases as humans. Apes and humans are both descended from a common hominoid ancestor which lived about 20 million years ago.

Until recently our knowledge of our earliest ancestors depended entirely on fossils. Fossilization is a rather hazardous process: under normal conditions most dead animals are quickly torn apart by scavengers and the scattered bones are soon broken down by the weather. Only if the animal's remains are quickly covered by sediments, for instance by being washed into a lake, do they stand any chance of being preserved and even then it is unusual for a whole skeleton to be fossilized. Large bones like skulls and long leg bones or smaller tough bones such as enamel-covered teeth are most likely to survive to become fossilized, but even these are quickly destroyed in the wet acid soils of tropical forests like those in which our hominoid ancestors lived.

Not surprisingly then, there are many gaps in the fossil record and it is not yet possible to reconstruct all the stages of our evolution from our earliest primate ancestors. In recent years some of these gaps have been, if not exactly filled in, illuminated by advances in DNA (deoxyribonucleic acid) sequencing. Put very simply, this technique allows the genetic make-up of different living species to be compared: the greater the differences, the longer the time that each species has been evolving separately. This "molecular clock" has made it possible to pinpoint with some accuracy the times at which the different branches of the hominoid family diverged and began their separate evolution; it has also dramatically emphasized just how closely we are related to the apes. Humans share an astonishing 98.4 percent of their genes with chimpanzees and only slightly fewer with the gorillas and orangutans. How much longer these close cousins will continue to share the planet with us is open to doubt: all are threatened with extinction as a result of human destruction of their habitat.

Darwin summarized the mechanism of evolution as "natural selection, or the survival of the fittest." New species evolve through the conservation of genetic mutations which enable an individual animal to survive more effectively. Such individuals are likely to enjoy greater success in reproduction and pass their genes on to a larger number of descendants. Over many generations genetic changes may accumulate to such a degree that a new species is formed. It is hard not to invest evolution with a sense of purpose: that of producing ever more refined life forms, becoming better adapted to their environments. Today humans dominate the Earth so completely that it is easy to assume that our evolution was inevitable because we are self-evidently the fittest. However, until relatively recently in geological time the possibility of the human race evolving was slim to say the least.

Human evolution, like that of every other living organism, began around 3.8 billion years ago, only 500 million years after the formation of the Earth. The first living things were simple single-celled organisms such as bacteria and algae. Life continued at this simple level for over 3 billion years until multi-celled plants and animals began to appear around 600 million years ago, shortly before the beginning of the Paleozoic era (550-225 million years ago). The first vertebrates – fishes – had evolved by 450 million

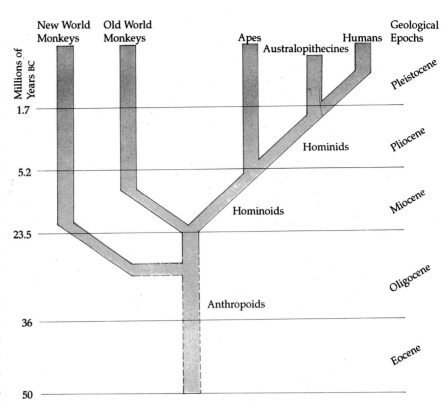

years ago, amphibians by 370 million, and reptiles by 280 million. Reptiles were the first vertebrate animals to be able to live their entire life cycles out of water and they evolved quickly to fill a wide range of unoccupied terrestrial environmental niches.

By the beginning of the Mesozoic era (225-65 million years ago), one group of reptiles had begun to develop mammal-like characteristics, such as warm-bloodedness and hair. At around the same time, the dinosaurs had begun to evolve from another group of reptiles. The dinosaurs were far more successful and efficient animals than the ancestral mammals, most of which could not compete with them and so became extinct. Those mammals which survived were small, even the largest were no bigger than a well-fed rat. Like small mammals today, such as voles and possums, they probably spent most of their lives under cover, feeding on insects, earthworms, fruit, seeds, and small reptiles. These small mammals would have been preyed upon by the smaller carnivorous dinosaurs and relied for survival on a fast breeding rate and on keeping a low profile. And so the mammals would no doubt always have remained but for the intervention of a 6-mile wide asteroid which smashed into what is now the Yucatán peninsula 65 million years ago. The resulting explosion wiped out almost all animal species larger than a cat, including all the dinosaurs.

When the dust settled, the surviving mammals found themselves largely without competitors and over the next 10 million

Above: A simplified evolutionary tree of the Old World monkeys, apes, and hominids. The ancestry of the New World monkeys is uncertain.

Far left: Before the development of the geological sciences in the nineteenth century, fossils were the subjects of folklore and superstition. Ammonites (*top left*), a common form of cephalod that flourished at the same time as the dinosaurs, were thought to be petrified snakes, eels, or ramshorns. Some American Indian tribes believed that trilobites (*bottom left*), an extinct relative of crabs and woodlice, could ward off evil spirits and give protection in battle. In medieval Europe fossils were believed to be the remains of animals that had drowned in the Biblical Flood.

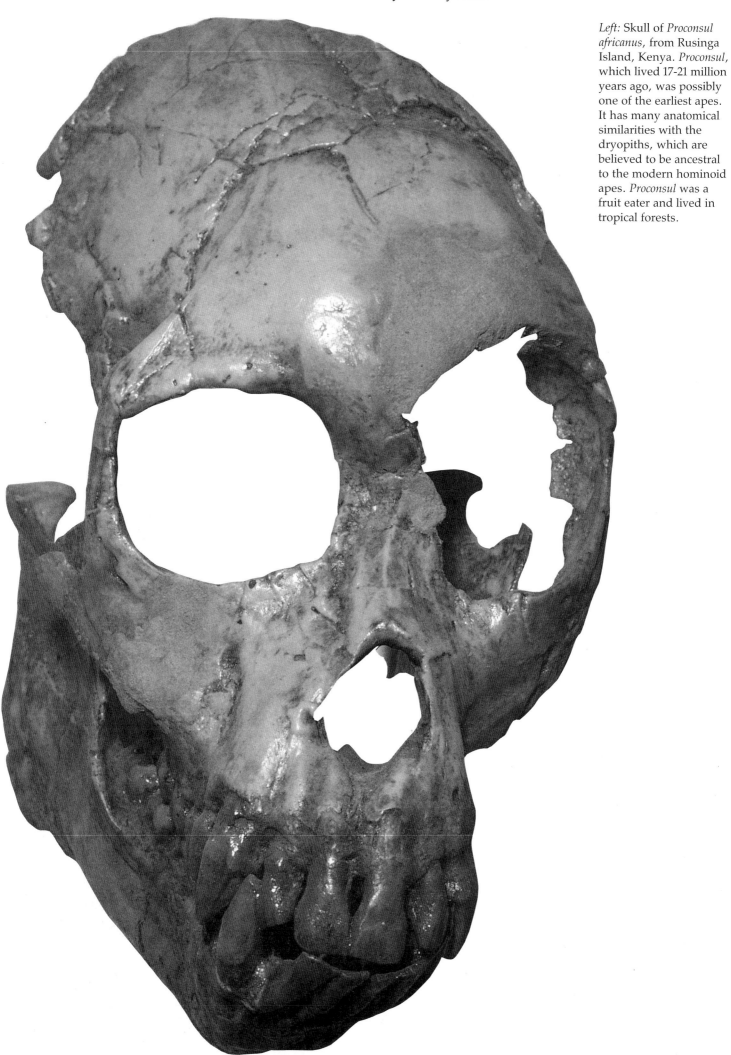

Left: Skull of *Proconsul africanus*, from Rusinga Island, Kenya. *Proconsul*, which lived 17-21 million years ago, was possibly one of the earliest apes. It has many anatomical similarities with the dryopiths, which are believed to be ancestral to the modern hominoid apes. *Proconsul* was a fruit eater and lived in tropical forests.

years or so they evolved rapidly to fill all of the environmental niches that the dinosaurs had occupied, as well as some – the sea for instance – that they had not. Our ancestors, the early primates, took to the trees. The best known of the early primates is *Plesiadapis* which lived across a wide area of North America and Europe in the Paleocene epoch, 65-53 million years ago. *Plesiadapis* was a little larger than a squirrel and had the strong dependence on vision and the flexible wrists and ankles typical of modern primates. However, *Plesiadapis* also had some unusual features which makes it unlikely to have been a direct ancestor of the modern primates, including, of course, ourselves. In the following epoch, the Eocene (53-35 million years ago), the first recognizably modern primates evolved. These had eyes at the front of their heads giving them the binocular vision which all modern primates possess. They also had nails rather than claws, and opposable fingers and toes which could grip branches and other objects. The first hominoid apes did not evolve until the Miocene epoch (25-5 million years ago). These early apes, known collectively as dryopiths, were all forest dwellers who spent most of their time in the trees and ate mostly fruit. The Miocene climate was warmer than that of the present day and tropical forests were much more widespread, so the dryopiths were able to spread over a wide area of Africa and Eurasia.

About 12 million years ago the world began to cool, a process which led eventually to the onset of the Ice Age about 1 million years ago. This global cooling was a disaster from which the apes, in terms of diversity of species, have never recovered. The cooler world was also drier causing the forests to shrink and give way to more open savannah and grassland, greatly reducing the apes' habitat and driving up to two-thirds of their species to extinction. Some of the dryopiths kept to an arboreal lifestyle and these formed the beginnings of the gibbon lineage. Others adapted to spend more time foraging for food on the ground and evolved into the group of Eurasian hominoids known as ramapiths. The ramapiths were knuckle-walkers, like gorillas and chimpanzees, and had strong jaws and large teeth with thick enamel which enabled them to include hard-to-chew foods like seeds and roots in their diet. Until very recently the best-known ramapith – *Ramapithecus* – was thought to be an early hominid (i.e. a proto-human) but most scientists now regard it as

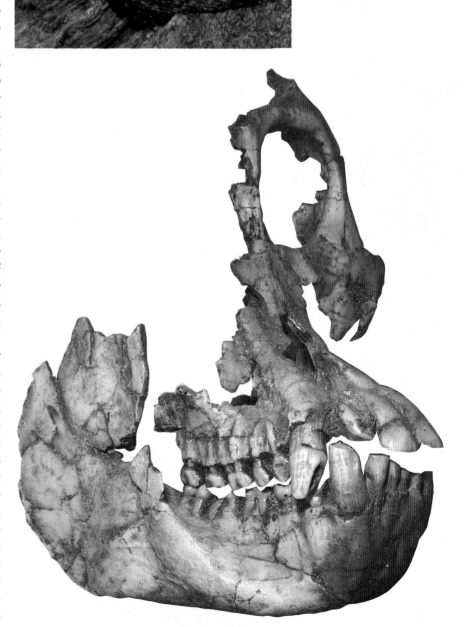

Left: The earliest primates were not unlike this modern Indian tree shrew in size, appearance, and lifestyle.

Below: The face and jaw of *Sivapithecus sivalensis* from the Potwar plateau, Pakistan. *Sivapithecus,* one of the commonest ramapiths, flourished in the Indian subcontinent around 8 million years ago. Until recently *Sivapithecus* was considered a possible human ancestor but it is now thought to be an ancestor of the orangutan.

being ancestral to the orangutan. Another ramapith was the spectacular *Gigantopithecus* which may have been around 9 feet tall and survived in Asia until as recently as 500,000 years ago. Some have suggested that *Gigantopithecus* was the ancestor of the Yeti and Bigfoot, though until someone actually manages to prove the existence of these semi-mythical beasts most scientists will continue to regard this as pretty wild speculation.

With *Ramapithecus* now removed from contention as a human ancestor, it remains unclear what was happening to the human-chimpanzee-gorilla lineage in the later Miocene: did it evolve from the ramapiths or separately from the dryopiths? Though fossil evidence is lacking, DNA sequencing has shown that the gorilla lineage split from the human-chimpanzee lineage about 6 million years ago, while humans and chimpanzees finally went their separate ways about 5 million years ago. About 1.5 million years ago the chimpanzee lineage also divided, into the common chimpanzee and the pygmy chimpanzee or bonobo. The split between the human and chimpanzee lineages was probably a result of the continuing climatic deterioration of the late Miocene. Some groups of the common human-chimpanzee ancestor probably found themselves isolated in ever-shrinking pockets of

forest in eastern Africa and were forced to adapt to life on the open savannahs or face extinction. Those groups of the common ancestor that lived in areas where forest cover was still extensive, as in West and Central Africa, faced no such pressures and evolved into the modern forest-dwelling chimpanzee.

What was the earliest hominid like and how did it behave? Probably the closest we can get to answering these questions is to take a look at the modern chimpanzee. The chimpanzee has a brain of about the same size as the earliest-known hominids, it still lives in a forest environment and it is also believed to have evolved less rapidly than humans and so is physically much more like our common ancestor than we are.

Chimpanzees are highly intelligent animals with complex social lives. Chimpanzee groups are hierarchical and characterized by constant power struggles between the dominant males who form alliances and indulge in subterfuge and planning to achieve their ends, chief of which is unchallenged access to sexually receptive females. Male chimpanzees are larger and stronger than the females and can physically dominate them. However "wooing" behavior, such as giving way to a female during feeding, is more common, especially among

Above: Mutual grooming helps cement social bonds in primate groups. Although only distantly related to humans, ground-living hamadryas baboons are thought to have a similar lifestyle to early hominids such as the australopithecines.

Right: All primates, including humans, show some degree of sexual dimorphism but it is most marked in gorillas. Male gorillas, like this silver-backed mountain gorilla from Zaire, may be up to twice the weight of a female. Though powerfully built, gorillas are not aggressive animals.

subordinate males who then need the co-operation of the female if they are to arrange a sexual encounter out of sight of the dominant male. Female common chimpanzees are sexually receptive for only a few days of their 46-day menstrual cycle and competition for females inspires much aggression among the males. Female bonobos are sexually receptive for up to eight times as long as those of the common chimpanzee and, with greater sexual opportunities for all, males are less aggressive to one another. Consequently, bonobos are able to live in much larger groups than common chimpanzees. Some anthropologists have drawn a parallel from this with the almost permanent sexual receptiveness of the human female and the human ability to live in large co-operative groups. Chimpanzee aggression is sometimes directed toward other chimpanzee groups and victory in a fight is often accompanied by the deliberate killing of the males of the defeated group: the human capacity for violence toward our own species is not unique but must have been inherent in our primate ancestors.

Though chimpanzees are mostly vegetarian, they do sometimes hunt monkeys for meat. Chimpanzee hunting strategy shows a remarkable degree of co-operation and forethought, and gives some idea of how early hominids may have taken up hunting. Chimpanzees are unable to catch monkeys by chasing them through the trees. Instead one chimpanzee acts as a driver while others station themselves on the likely line of flight and ambush the fleeing monkey. The meat is shared out afterward between the whole group: food-sharing is, of course, an important aspect of human behavior too.

The human capacity for planned migration may also be a consequence of our ape ancestry. In chimpanzee groups it is common for groups of subordinate males to forage for food separately from the main group in order to keep out of the way of the dominant male. These groups can cover a wide area and play an important role in discovering new food sources. The males do not keep their discoveries to themselves but pass the knowledge on to the main group. This means they have to share the food but it also increases their status with the females. If the new food source is rich enough the group may migrate and establish itself permanently in the new territory. It is quite

Above: Tool use was once thought to be an exclusively human achievement but it is now known that chimpanzees make and use a range of simple tools. Here a young female is using a stick to dig for roots or grubs. The earliest hominids may have used similar tools.

Right: Chimpanzees are our closest living relations in the animal world, sharing with us 98.4 percent of the same genes. Like humans, chimpanzees are highly intelligent and enjoy complex social lives and strong family bonds.

possible that early hominids increased their ranges in a similar way. As their intelligence increased, the early hominids became more able to turn this behavior into a deliberate quest for new habitats to exploit.

As with humans, chimpanzees are born at a relatively early stage of development and require intensive nurturing. Mother-child (especially mother-son) bonds are normally very strong and where for some reason they are not, the young chimpanzee grows up to be socially maladjusted and incapable of forming normal relationships with other chimpanzees. Females with problem upbringings are themselves likely to be unsuccessful mothers. Young chimps must learn much of their behavior from the group's adults, including food sources, social and communication skills, and tool use – once thought to be a uniquely human attribute. Common chimp tools include rocks used for cracking nuts, bundles of leaves used like sponges for drawing drinking water out of awkward crevices and for washing, and sticks used for extracting termites from their nests (gorillas are intelligent enough to use tools but when they fancy a snack of termites they just smash a hole in the nest). Rocks suitable for nutcracking are scarce through most of the chimps' range and such rocks are carefully stored and sometimes carried from site to site. Chimps can be quite possessive and clearly have some sense of ownership of "their" rocks. Chimps that do not possess suitable rocks for nutcracking will literally beg, borrow, or steal them from others. Under laboratory conditions chimps have even been taught to make and use simple flake tools by breaking rocks. This, the height of chimp technological achievement, falls well short of the earliest-known hominid tools but it is probable that early hominids went through a similar stage of using natural objects as tools before learning to manufacture them. Indeed it is quite possible that the common human-chimp ancestor already used simple tools 5 million years ago. Chimps also have a limited capacity for abstract symbolic thought and have been taught to talk using sign language up to the level of a two-and-a-half-year-old human child.

There are clearly limits to the conclusions which can safely be drawn about early hominid behavior by studying chimpanzees: after all, chimps are not humans. However, few could fail to recognize something of ourselves in them, and it is likely that our earliest hominid ancestors were not significantly different.

CHAPTER TWO
Southern Apes and Handy Men

The most important physical differences between humans and apes are our erect bipedal way of walking, our large brains, our flexible hands, and our distinctive dentition and jaws. Some of these characteristics cause human beings some physical disadvantages so, in evolutionary terms, the advantages these characteristics brought our ancestors must have been great indeed. Bipedalism limits the speed at which humans can run, making them more vulnerable to predators. The adaptation of our feet to walking bipedaly means that we have lost the apes' ability to grip with our feet, making us indifferent tree climbers. Bipedalism also requires a narrow pelvis and this severely limits the size of the birth canal in females: as a result humans have a far higher chance of suffering fatal complications during childbirth than any other mammal. The adaptation of the human spine to bipedalism remains incomplete: we would have far fewer back problems if we still walked on all fours.

Large brains are an expensive luxury in a physiological sense as they require a large blood and energy supply, diverting the body's resources away from the muscles. Most animals manage very adequately without large brains and even chimpanzees, our closest competitors in the brain-size stakes, have less than a third of the human brain capacity. The small size of the human female's birth canal also means that a human child must be born while its brain is still small and underdeveloped. A new-born human's brain is only 25 percent of its adult size, compared to 46 percent for a new-born chimpanzee. Consequently human infants

Below: The skull and (*below left*) the dental arcade of a robust australopithecine from Olduvai Gorge, Tanzania. The massive jaws and molars show that they lived on a diet of tough vegetable matter. Though they were bipedal, robust australopithecines are not thought to be direct human ancestors.

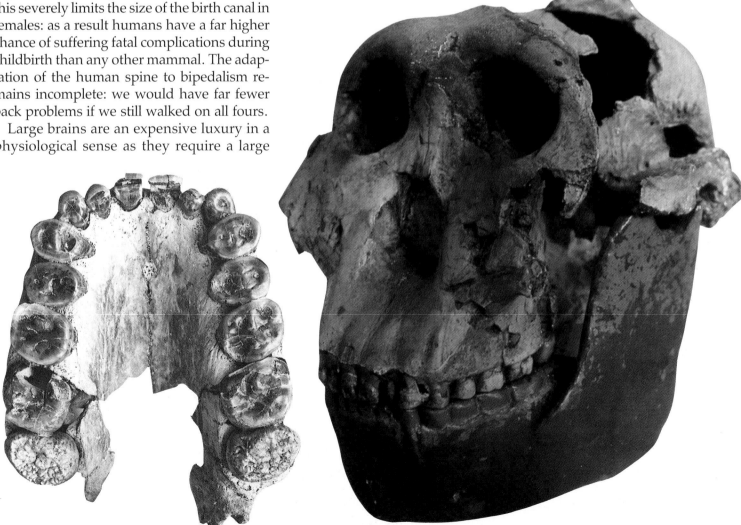

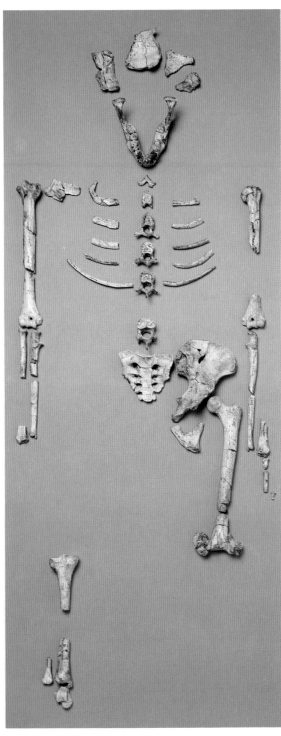

larynx, the "voice box" which enables us to speak, also makes it easy for humans to choke to death while eating.

For a long time it was widely assumed that all the distinctive features of modern humans evolved in parallel at a constant rate. By the 1950s, however, fossil evidence indicated that human-like dentition had evolved before human-like brains. If teeth and brains could evolve out of sync then so too could bipedalism. Just how far the evolution of bipedalism was out of sync was dramatically demonstrated by one of the most exciting finds in the search for our origins. In 1974 a 40 percent complete skeleton of a

Far left: One of the most important anthropological discoveries of all time: a 3.5 million-year-old skeleton of *Australopithecus afarensis*, better known as "Lucy," from Hadar, Ethiopia. This discovery proved that humans had evolved bipedal locomotion almost 2 million years before they evolved large brains. Lucy's brain was only the size of a chimpanzee's but her hip, leg, and knee bones showed that she was fully adapted to bipedalism.

Left: An artist's reconstruction of Lucy as she might have looked in life.

are particularly helpless and demand an enormous investment of care by their parents over many years while their brains develop.

Humans have shorter jaws than apes and smaller canine teeth. Human teeth are set in a distinctive elliptical arcade (the dental arcades of apes are shaped more like three sides of a rectangle) and have thicker enamel than ape teeth, making it easy to distinguish an early hominid from an ape by its teeth alone. The short human jaw is responsible for the acute discomfort which the eruption of our wisdom teeth causes many of us and means that there is a wide range of foods that we cannot eat without processing them first. The unique structure of the human

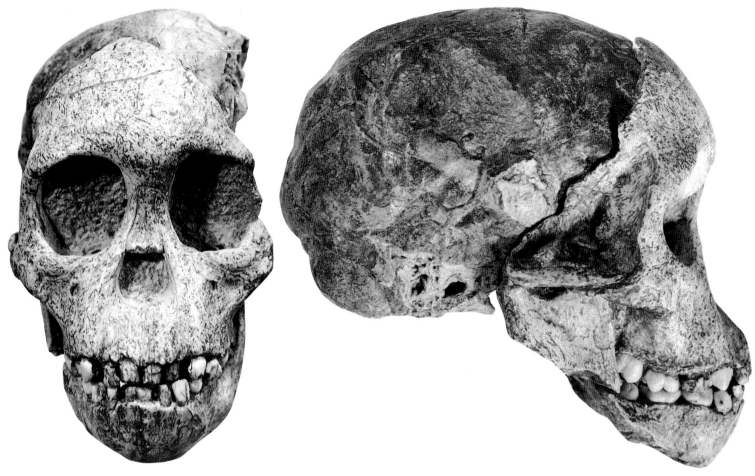

small female hominid in 3.5 million-year-old sediments was discovered at Afar in Ethiopia. Given the scientific name of *Australopithecus afarensis* ("southern ape of Afar"), she is much better known as Lucy after the Beatles' song "Lucy in the Sky with Diamonds" which was being played in the expedition's camp on the day of her discovery. Lucy was just over 3 feet tall, had long arms, and weighed about as much as a chimpanzee. Her brain capacity was just 25 cubic inches, almost identical to that of a chimpanzee. However, her hip, leg bones, and knee joints showed beyond doubt that Lucy had been bipedal; Lucy's gait was not identical to a modern human's but it was not inferior in efficiency. Lucy, the earliest hominid discovered until 1994, was a fully adapted biped with no more brains than a chimpanzee. In fact Lucy predates the first large-brained hominids by 2 million years.

In 1975-76 the remains of up to 13 more specimens of *Australopithecus afarensis* were found at a single site in the same area. It is thought that they may have been victims of a flash flood. This group included males, females, and infants and was quickly dubbed the "First Family." This discovery revealed that *Australopithecus afarensis* showed marked sexual dimorphism (i.e. difference in size between the sexes): as with the gorilla and many other primates the

male was much larger than the female. In 1976 further evidence that early hominids were bipedal was discovered at Laetoli in Tanzania when the footprints of two adult and one infant hominid were found in a bed of volcanic ash 3.6 million years old. A nearby volcano had blasted the fine gray ash out over the surrounding countryside. Shortly afterward the three hominids – the two adults walking in single file, the child skipping around more erratically – passed through leaving their footprints behind them in the soft ash. Rain later soaked the ash and as it dried out it set like concrete, preserving the footprints. Analysis of casts of the footprints has shown that these hominids, perhaps *Australopithecus afarensis*, had feet that were very similar indeed to those of modern humans.

Lucy was no more intelligent than a chimpanzee, so bipedalism is unlikely to have been an adaptation to free the hands for more effective toolmaking. In any case, there is no evidence that *Australopithecus afarensis* made tools. Why then did the early hominids adapt to bipedalism? The answer probably has something to do with climate change. The chimpanzee-hominid lineage divided about 5 million years ago, at the end of the Miocene epoch. In the following epoch, the Pliocene (5-1.5 million years ago), the global cooling which had begun in the

Above: Two views of the Taung skull, a juvenile gracile australopithecine which lived near Johannesburg, South Africa, over 2 million years ago. After death the child's brain cavity filled with mineral-rich liquids which crystalized forming a perfect mold or "endocast" of the inside of the skull. This has preserved the shape and some of the structures of the child's brain. Though very ape-like in size and structure, the child's brain has better developed frontal lobes than either the gorilla or chimpanzee.

Miocene continued and with it the continued drying out of the African continent and the shrinking of its forests. In East Africa, which fossil evidence points to as the birthplace of the hominids, the drying effect was probably exacerbated by the geological upheavals that led to the uplift of the East African plateau and the great East African Rift Valley. The hominoid apes of the region would have been split up into isolated groups as their habitat shrank to form "islands" of forest. Such conditions are ideal for the evolution of new species as genetic changes can spread very quickly through a small breeding population where they might be swallowed up in a large one.

Imagine a group of hominoids living in a shrinking island of forest and increasingly short of food. A genetic mutation gives one of the males slightly longer legs which enables it to forage more widely in the surrounding grassland: it finds more food, is better nourished and stronger than the other males; it becomes the dominant male and fathers more offspring, many of whom inherit the advantageous gene for longer legs. These offspring will also do better than other apes without the gene and will in turn enjoy greater breeding success. In a small group it takes only a few generations for the whole population to acquire the advantageous long-leg gene. If environmental pressures remain the same and foraging in open country continues to bring significant benefits, then any further genetic variation resulting in still longer legs will also quickly establish itself in the population. In time, a new species will arise, characterized not only by the physical difference of having longer legs but also by a different way of life involving extensive foraging in open country: in fact this may become the normal way of life for the species.

In reality, the evolution of the hominids as a distinct family is likely to have been a great deal more complicated than this speculative reconstruction. For example, teeth and jaws also had to change to cope with a diet that included tough seeds and roots which formed the main food source of the grasslands. The thick enamel which is a characteristic of hominid teeth was probably an adaptation to this kind of tooth-wearing diet. At some point too, though not at once, larger brains became an advantage to the hominids.

Why did hominids adapt to living in a more open savannah-type habitat by becoming bipedal when no other animal has done so? Even other primates like baboons, which

have adapted to a savannah habitat, have done so by evolving a more efficient quadrupedal gait. Plant foods on the savannah are of poorer quality than those found in forests, so the early hominids would have needed to be able to cover a wider range than their forest-dwelling forebears. Thus, bipedalism would have allowed the hominids to do this in an energy-efficient way and at the same time raised their eye level above the grass to give them a good all-round view. It has also been argued that bipedalism helped hominids avoid overheating on the dry hot savannahs. An erect walking position exposes only 40 percent of the body area to the direct heat of the sun compared to a more exposed quadrupedal position. Thus bipedalism may have allowed hominids to forage at times of the day when most of their competitors were lying up in the shade. Sweat glands and loss of body hair may be another adaptation to an open habitat. That bipedalism freed the hands to carry and throw objects and make tools was initially incidental to these advantages, only later did these characteristics show their potential.

Lucy's species, *Australopithecus afarensis*, was, as we have seen, already fully adapted

Below: A simplified evolutionary tree of the hominids. Though *Australopithecus afarensis* is generally accepted as a human ancestor, the relationship of the other australopithecines to the human line is still uncertain. The position of the gracile australopithecine *Australopithecus africanus* is particularly unclear: was it a direct human ancestor or did humans evolve from *Australopithecus afarensis* through other, undiscovered, intermediaries?

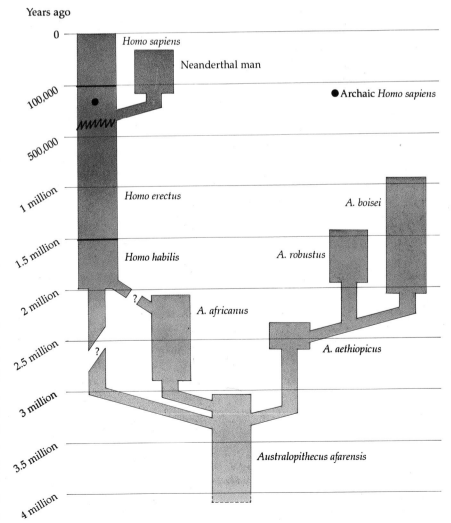

Years ago

to bipedalism 3.5 million years ago, so it is likely that the transition from quadrupedalism or knuckle-walking took place before 4 million years ago. How long before we still cannot say. The earliest-known hominid, *Australopithecus ramidus*, which lived around 4.4 million years ago, is known only from the upper parts of its skeleton. The shape of the skull suggests that it was balanced on top of the spine as in later bipedal hominids but *Australopithecus ramidus* also had relatively long arms and ape-like teeth, suggesting that it may have been primarily a forest dweller still adapted for tree climbing.

Australopithecus afarensis became extinct about 3 million years ago and was replaced by two types of australopithecine: a "gracile" form, *Australopithecus africanus*, and a number of "robust" forms. The terms "gracile" and "robust" refer not to body size but to their teeth and jaws which are thought to be signs of dietary specialization. The robust australopithecines had massive jaws and large molars suitable for grinding tough plant foods. The smaller teeth and jaws of *Australopithecus africanus* are thought to be a sign that its diet was more varied and may have even included meat scavenged from carcasses. The craniums of the robust australopithecines had a prominent crest of bone which acted as an anchor for powerful jaw muscles: the gracile australopithecines, with their smaller jaws, did not have this cranial crest. The australopithecines were very successful animals and appear to have been as common in eastern and southern

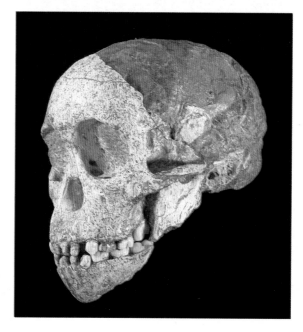

Above: A drier and cooler climate caused the East African forests to shrink in the late Pliocene epoch, forcing the early hominids to spend more time on the ground in open country like the savannah of Tanzania's Serengeti plain.

Center: Reconstruction of the skull of the gracile australopithecine *Australopithecus africanus* from South Africa (*c.* 1.5 million years old). The terms "gracile" and "robust" refer to the size of the jaws and teeth: compare this skull with that on page 20. The smaller teeth and jaws of *Australopithecus africanus* suggest it had a more varied diet than robust australopithecines, possibly including some meat.

Left: Another view of the Taung skull.

Africa as baboons are today. The robust australopithecines, which are not believed to be direct human ancestors, survived until around 1 million years ago when they became extinct. *Australopithecus africanus* did not last nearly so long and disappeared over 2 million years ago, about the same time that the first hominid to be given the title "*Homo*" – *Homo habilis* – appeared.

Homo habilis had a body very like that of an australopithecine, with relatively long arms and slightly curled toes suggesting that it was a good climber. *Homo habilis*' skull, though, shows major differences from the australopithecine's. It still has a pronounced brow ridge above the eyes but the teeth are much smaller than any species of *Australopithecus*, while *Homo habilis*' brain is much larger and had a more human shape and structure. The australopithecines had brains which were slightly larger than a chimpanzee's but still less than a third of the size of a

Above: The robust australopithecine *Australopithecus robustus*. The prominent crest on top of the skull was an anchor for the powerful muscles that worked its massive jaws.

Left: Partial skull of *Homo habilis* from Sterkfontaine, South Africa. *Homo habilis*, the earliest form of human, first appeared around 2 million years ago and has a much larger brain than the australopithecines. *Homo habilis* probably evolved from the gracile australopithecines.

modern human's: *Homo habilis* had a brain which was almost half the size. The skull shape is also more modern and lacks the characteristic crest of the robust australopithecines' skulls. Paleoanthropologists are still uncertain as to *Homo habilis'* origins, but it is generally held to have evolved from the gracile australopithecines.

Homo habilis gets its name, which means "handy man," because its appearance roughly coincides with the appearance of the first stone artifacts 2.4 million years ago. The most typical of these artifacts are so-called choppers: pebbles which have had a few flakes trimmed off one edge to make a rough cutting edge. The sharp-edged flakes were once thought to have been waste products but these were actually used as cutting tools. Unmodified pebbles were used as hammer stones, and sticks and bones may have been used as digging sticks to obtain roots. This simple toolmaking technology is known as the Oldowan after Olduvai Gorge, the site in Tanzania where the tools were first recognized. Though simple, these tools are a sign that *Homo habilis'* large brain gave it powers of visualization, planning, and prediction which were much more advanced than those found in modern apes. As its tools are often found in association with fossil animal bones, *Homo habilis* is also the first hominid known to eat meat as a normal part of its diet. The Oldowan marks the beginning of the Old Stone Age or Paleolithic, the longest period of human prehistory, which lasted until the end of the Ice Age, 10,000 years ago. The Paleolithic has three subdivisions defined by changes in human technology: the Lower Paleolithic (2.5 million-150,000 years ago), the Middle (150,000-40,000), and Upper (40,000-10,000).

The impetus behind these revolutionary physical and behavioral changes was probably the beginning of extreme climatic instability about 2.5 million years ago. Generally the climate became colder. Large ice caps began to form in Antarctica and the Arctic Ocean froze over. Africa became even drier and less forested. In these testing conditions natural selection would favor an intelligent animal with opportunist and flexible behavior patterns: meat-eating and toolmaking together greatly enlarged the potential food sources available to the hominids on the open plains.

There has been a great deal of controversy over the way of life of this earliest human. Some have seen *Homo habilis* as a quite sophisticated hunter-gatherer bringing food

Opposite page, left: This skull from Lake Turkana, Kenya, illustrates the difficulties of classifying hominid fossils: anthropologists are uncertain as to whether it is a gracile australopithecine or a form of *Homo habilis.*

Below: Finding a fossil of an early human is often the least part of an anthropologist's difficulties. Reconstructing and interpreting the fragmentary remains of this 1.8 million-year-old mature *Homo habilis* female from Tanzania took months of painstaking work. She was less than 4 feet tall and much more ape-like than anthropologists had previously thought *Homo habilis* to have been.

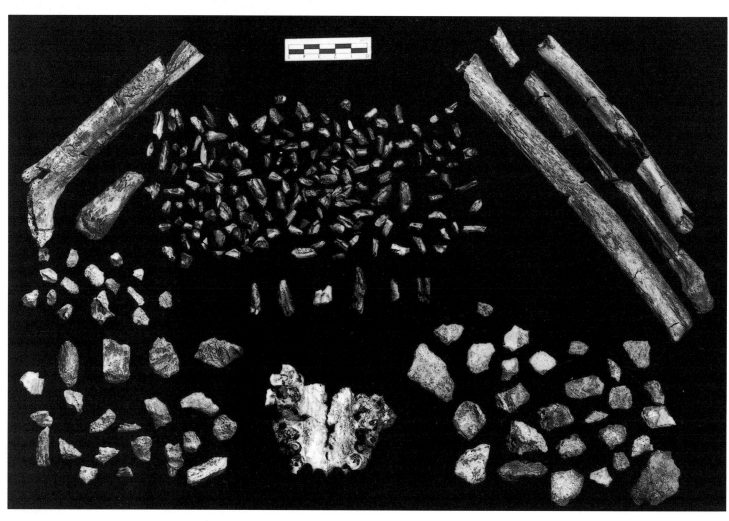

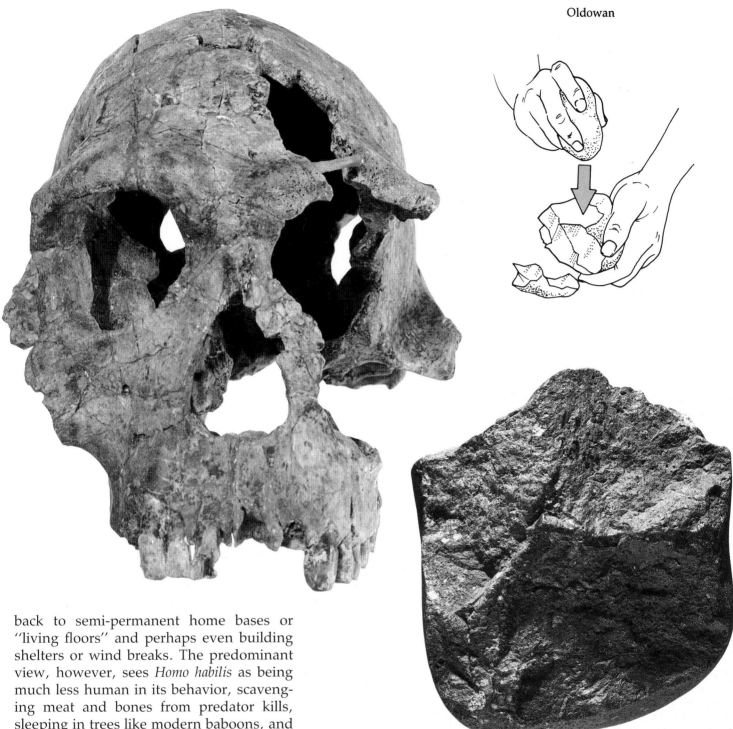

Oldowan

back to semi-permanent home bases or "living floors" and perhaps even building shelters or wind breaks. The predominant view, however, sees *Homo habilis* as being much less human in its behavior, scavenging meat and bones from predator kills, sleeping in trees like modern baboons, and relying more on muscle power than tool use (*Homo habilis* was at least as strong as an adult chimpanzee which is capable of tearing off a human's arm).

Those who support the "scavenging hypothesis" argue that *Homo habilis* would not have needed to have been an active hunter to include meat in its diet. The East African savannah supports vast herds of herbivores, some of which die of natural causes and many more of which are killed by predators like lions. After the predators have eaten their fill there is usually plenty left over for scavengers like hyenas and wild dogs but, despite their powerful jaws, they would have had difficulty getting at the brains and the nutritious marrow in the long

leg bones. By using its simple tools to break open skulls and leg bones, *Homo habilis* could exploit a food source for which there was effectively no competition. If *Homo habilis* was lucky enough to reach a carcass before the hyenas, it could use its tools to cut through the toughest hide and slice meat off the bones quickly and carry it away to be eaten in the safety of a tree. Simple though they were, modern experiments have shown that Oldowan tools are quite adequate even to butcher an elephant. Indeed, many fossil elephant bones have been found which show tell-tale cut marks made by *Homo habilis*' stone tools during butchery.

Top right: The Oldowan toolmaking technique used by *Homo habilis* simply involved striking a few flakes off a pebble of hard, easily splintered rock. The sharp flakes were used for cutting meat off bones and the core or "chopper" probably for breaking open marrow bones.

Above right: An Oldowan chopper tool from Olduvai Gorge, Tanzania.

CHAPTER THREE
The First Hunters

Homo habilis flourished for about half a million years then, about 1.6 million years ago, it was abruptly replaced by a new, even larger-brained, hominid species: *Homo erectus* (erect or upright man), the first hominid known to have lived outside Africa. *Homo erectus* was the most successful human species, surviving for almost 1.5 million years: our species, *Homo sapiens*, has so far survived only about 100,000 years. The first specimens of *Homo erectus*, discovered in Java in 1891 and China in 1929, were around 700,000 years old and were at that time the oldest hominids known. Though Darwin predicted that Africa would be the best place to look for the fossil evidence of the human race's earliest ancestors, these discoveries seemed to confirm the view of many nineteenth-century anthropologists that Asia, the traditional location of the Biblical Garden of Eden, was the birthplace of humanity. However, discoveries of similar fossils in East Africa in the 1960s and 1970s which predated the Asian specimens by as much as 1 million years, apparently established Africa as the birthplace of the human race. Recent re-dating of some of the *erectus* finds from Java to between 1.6 and 1.8 million years ago – as old as, or older than, the oldest African *erectus* fossils – has

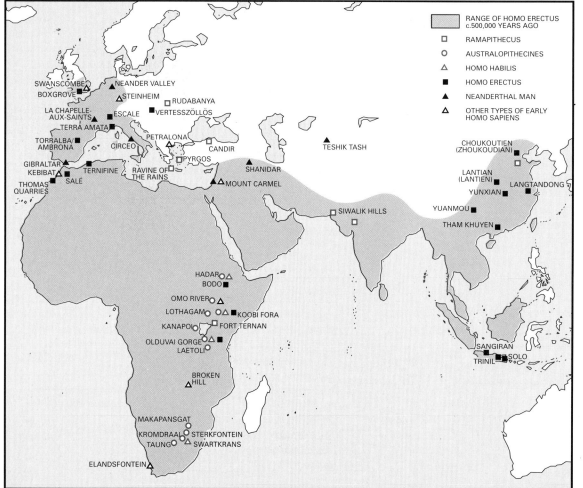

Above right: Cast of the skull of Peking Man, a 700,000-year-old example of *Homo erectus* from Choukoutien near Peking. At the time of its discovery in 1929, Peking Man was the oldest-known hominid and was taken as evidence that humans had evolved in Asia rather than Africa. The original fossil was lost during World War II.

Left: Map showing the distribution of fossil hominids. The ramapith apes were distributed widely through Africa and Eurasia, but the earliest hominids – the australopithecines and *Homo habilis* – are found only in Africa. *Homo erectus* was the first hominid to be widely distributed outside Africa.

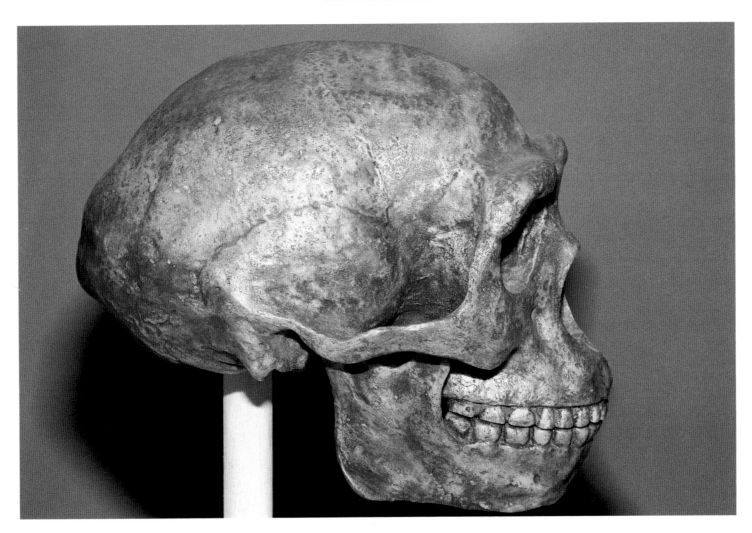

renewed the controversy. These dates are not universally accepted at present but if they are confirmed, many of our present ideas about *Homo erectus* will have to be rethought.

Homo erectus had a brain which varied from about two-thirds the size of a modern human's brain in the earlier specimens to over three-fourths in later examples. However, the *erectus* brain lacked the highly developed frontal lobes that are such an outstanding feature of the modern human brain. The difference can be seen very clearly from the flask shape of the skull when seen from above – broad at the back but narrowing considerably toward the front. *Homo erectus* still had a prominent brow ridge above the eyes and with its low forehead and protruding jaw it would have retained a somewhat ape-like appearance. The palate and the base of the skull suggest that *Homo erectus* had a less evolved larynx than modern humans and though it could probably communicate using a wide range of sounds it was probably not capable of speech as we would recognize it. From the neck down *Homo erectus* was, to all intents and purposes, a fully modern human. The only noticeable difference was that *Homo erectus* was slightly taller and better built than modern humans.

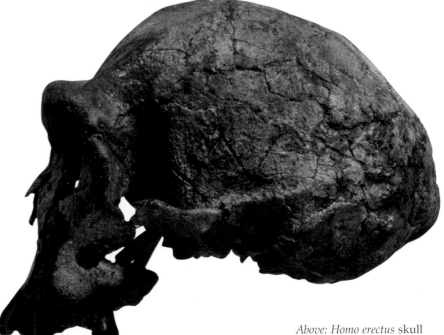

An almost complete skeleton of a 12-year-old *erectus* boy found at Lake Turkana in Kenya in 1984 had a height of 5 feet 5 inches. Estimates based on this find suggesting that an adult *erectus* would have averaged 6 feet tall were confirmed recently by the discovery of adult *erectus* leg bones at Boxgrove in southern England which also pointed to a height

Above: Homo erectus skull from Lake Turkana, Kenya, dated to 1.6-1.2 million years old. The discovery in the 1960s in East Africa of fossils of *Homo erectus* that predated Asian specimens by a million years seemed to confirm Africa as the birthplace of the human race.

of about 6 feet. Late examples of *Homo erectus* have very variable features but are generally less well-built and have more modern facial features and larger brains. Consequently, late *Homo erectus* is difficult to distinguish from early *Homo sapiens* and is sometimes termed "archaic *Homo sapiens*" in recognition of its transitional appearance.

The appearance of *Homo erectus* coincides with the appearance of a new and more sophisticated toolmaking tradition known as the Acheulean after the site in northern France where it was first identified. The most striking Acheulean tool is the symmetrical handax, an efficient butchery tool, but *Homo erectus* also made a wide range of other tools such as cleavers, scrapers, and borers. The Acheulean technology demonstrates a huge advance in *erectus'* mental abilities over *Homo habilis*. To make a handax, a good spatial imagination is required to visualize the shape of the tool within the unworked rock. While a chopper tool was the more or less accidental result of knocking a few cutting flakes off a cobble, a handax requires dozens of well thought out and precisely administered blows: it is not a skill that a modern human would find easy to acquire.

Homo erectus was the first hominid to use fire. The earliest evidence of the hominid use of fire is from Swartkrans in South Africa and Chesowanya in Kenya and dates from 1.6 million years ago. At this time *Homo erectus* probably relied on natural bush fires as a source of fire but presumably had learned

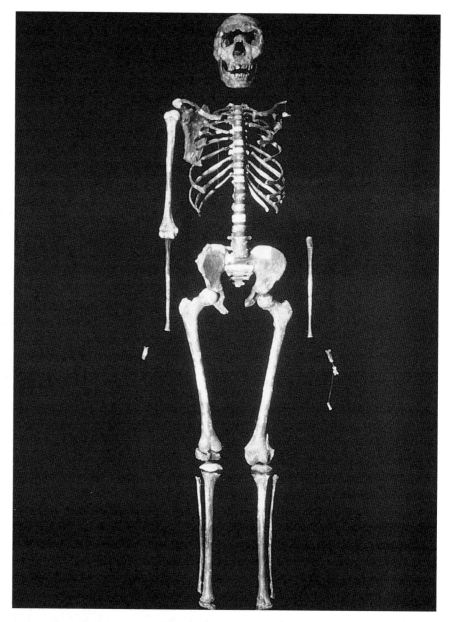

Above: Homo erectus was taller and stronger than modern humans. This skeleton of a 12-year-old *Homo erectus* boy from Lake Turkana, Kenya, is 5 feet 5 inches tall. Had he lived to adulthood, he would have grown to around 6 feet tall. At 1.6 million years old this is the oldest securely dated *Homo erectus* fossil yet known.

Left: Homo erectus was probably the first hominid to build shelters. This is a reconstruction of the remains of a simple hut built at Terra Amata in southern France around 380,000 years ago.

how to start a fire artificially by the time it moved out of Africa into the colder regions of Asia and Europe where fire would have been essential to survival. The move out of Africa also implies that *erectus* could make clothes and build shelters. What are claimed to be the remains of a 300,000-year-old brushwood hut have been found at Terra Amata in southern France. This was a flimsy structure and would not have been draft-proof unless it had been covered with hides.

Though *Homo erectus*, like *Homo habilis*, probably continued to get most of its meat by scavenging, it was also the first hominid actively to hunt for meat. Evidence from Torralba and Ambrona in Spain suggests that the main hunting tactic was to drive animals, even ones as large as elephants and rhinoceroses, into traps such as swamps where they would become enmired and could be easily killed. Though *erectus* used sharpened sticks as spears, it did not use the bow and arrow or the spear thrower, nor did it make stone spearheads. This makes it un-likely that *erectus* hunted by stalking as it would have had to get very close indeed to its prey to have much chance of scoring a disabling hit. Perhaps its physical strength allowed *erectus* to run down prey that a modern human could never catch?

The evolution of *Homo erectus* can be seen as further hominid adaptation to an increas-ingly challenging environment. By the beginning of the Pleistocene epoch 1.5 million years ago, the world was beginning to enter the Ice Age. The Ice Age was a period of extreme climatic instability. Long periods of intense cold known as glacials alternated with shorter periods known as interglacials when the climate was as warm or warmer than that of the present day. During glacial periods huge ice sheets formed on the northern continents causing sea levels to fall by up to 450 feet in the col-dest periods. The African climate became very arid and forests retreated into small pockets called refugia. Though areas close to the equator did not cool down as much as areas closer to the poles, upland areas in Africa would still have been cold enough at times to cause a tropically adapted animal

Above: The tools most commonly associated with *Homo erectus* are symmetrical handaxes such as these from Abbeville-St Acheul in northern France. Despite their name, handaxes were probably used as heavy-duty butchery knives.

Below left: Homo erectus toolmakers discovered that using a bone hammer, rather than another stone, allowed them to strike flakes with greater precision to make more sophisticated tools than *Homo habilis*. This toolmaking technique is known as the Acheulean after the site in France where it was first identified.

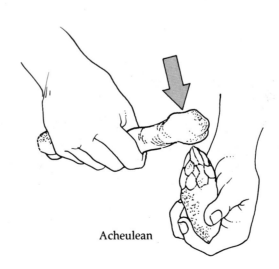

Acheulean

ago. There are two possible routes which *erectus* could have used to leave Africa. The first possibility is that *erectus* bands followed game northward along the course of the Nile into Egypt and spread from there into the Near East and North Africa about 900,000 years ago. By 500,000 years ago *Homo erectus* had spread across Europe as far north as Britain. As there is no evidence to suggest that *Homo erectus* knew how to make boats, it is more likely that it reached Europe via the Near East and Anatolia than by crossing the Mediterranean from North Africa. Ice Age Europe was dominated by steppe grass-lands which blended into tundra in the north. Though *Homo erectus* could not cope with the subarctic tundra, the temperate steppes provided it with an environment which was in many ways similar to that of the African savannah in that it supported large herds of grazing animals, such as deer, horse, wild cattle, and elephants. Keeping warm in winter was a problem but fire solved that. If *erectus* still relied on scavenging to a great extent, winter may actually have been a good time of year. The death rate among herd animals is highest in winter and with the cold helping to preserve the animals' carcasses there may actually have been more food available then than in the summer.

Left: It is probable that many early hominids made and used wooden tools but very few have survived. Dated to 200,000 years ago, this wooden spear point (or perhaps a snow-probe) from Clacton, England, is the oldest wooden tool to have survived.

Below: Homo erectus skull from Koobi Fora, Lake Turkana, Kenya, showing the characteristic heavy bone ridges around the eye sockets.

discomfort. During interglacials, wetter conditions prevailed, forests spread and sea levels rose at times above modern levels. The transition between glacial and interglacial conditions could be very rapid, taking only a few decades. It was this variability rather than the cold of the glacial periods that made the Pleistocene a difficult time for many animal species besides *Homo erectus*: an animal had to be able to adapt quickly to environmental changes or become extinct. In these circumstances an ability to adapt flexibly to changing conditions by behavioral changes – such as improved tool manufacture, use of fire, co-operative hunting tactics and so on – would create a powerful selective pressure in favor of increased brain size.

Especially after it mastered fire, the glacial periods were far more favorable to *Homo erectus* than might be imagined, as it was far easier for a scavenger and hunter to make a living on the game-filled savannahs than it was in a tropical forest with plentiful vegetable foods but few large mammals. The low sea levels also helped *Homo erectus* to spread over a wider range than any previous hominid. It is thought that *Homo erectus* began to move out of East Africa about 1 million years

The second route out of Africa would only have been open when sea levels were lowered during glacial periods. During these periods it would have been possible for *Homo erectus* bands to walk across the bed of the Red Sea to Arabia. From Arabia it would have been possible to walk from the Horn of Africa across the Persian Gulf into India and eventually to China and Southeast Asia which *erectus* had reached by about 700,000 years ago. During glacial periods most of the Indonesian islands were linked to the Southeast Asian mainland by land bridges, so *Homo erectus* was able to get as far as Java without getting its feet wet but this was the end of the line. *Erectus* could not make boats and Australia and New Guinea remained unpopulated. Though America was linked to Asia during glacial periods by a land bridge across the Bering Sea, *Homo erectus* did not get there as the arctic environment was too hostile.

Though the European and Near Eastern *erectus* populations used Acheulean handaxes, the Chinese and Southeast Asian populations used stone tools which were scarcely an advance on the Oldowan tools used by *Homo habilis*. This does not mean that East Asian *erectus* was in any way degenerate: it is likely that it relied to a great extent on bamboo, a highly versatile material which can be used to make razor-sharp knives and projectile points but which soon decays leaving no traces for the archeologist to uncover. Excavations of caves at Choukoutien, near Peking,

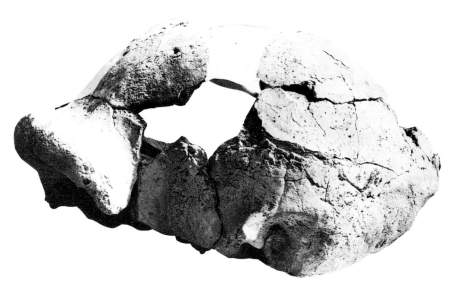

suggest that Asian *erectus* was a resourceful hunter, preying on 60 different species of animal from deer to bats.

The isolated populations of *erectus* formed by its spread across Eurasia seem to have begun to evolve in separate directions around 500,000 years ago. Though all had a tendency to develop larger brains, Asian *erectus* was evolutionarily the most conservative and still survived relatively unchanged as late as 230,000 years ago. In Africa, *erectus* appears to have evolved gradually into anatomically modern *Homo sapiens* by around 135,000 years ago. In Europe *Homo erectus* went through a period of great physical variability after 300,000 years ago, but by 230,000 years ago it had evolved into Neanderthal man.

Above: Homo erectus cranium from Olduvai Gorge, Tanzania. *Homo erectus's* cranium has been described as flask-shaped as it is widest at the back and narrowest at the front.

Left: In Africa *Homo erectus* evolved gradually through intermediate forms known as archaic *Homo sapiens* into anatomically modern *Homo sapiens* between 500,000 and 130,000 years ago. ''Rhodesian Man'' from Kabwe, Zambia, is such an intermediate form. The skull still has the brow ridges, prognathous jaw, and low-vaulted cranium of *Homo erectus* but the brain capacity is the same as a modern human's.

CHAPTER FOUR

The Mysterious Neanderthals

Neanderthal man has a problem: nobody seems to know what to make of him. Was Neanderthal man an ancestor of modern humans or was he a side branch of the main human line that led to an evolutionary dead end? Was he dim and brutish or would we recognize his behavior as being intelligent, sophisticated, and fully human? Some of the first specimens of Neanderthal man to be discovered were wildly misinterpreted. A partial skeleton found in a cave in the Neander valley near Düsseldorf, Germany, in 1856 was first thought to be that of a Cossack who had crawled into the cave to die during the Napoleonic Wars: later its oddly shaped skull led to its reinterpretation as a mental defective.

Only in 1864 was Neanderthal man recognized as a species of prehistoric human. The discovery of a largely complete Neanderthal skeleton at La Chapelle-aux-Saints in France in 1908 led to the first scientific attempts to reconstruct Neanderthal man's appearance. Unfortunately, it was not fully recognized that this was the skeleton of an old man who had been crippled and disfigured by arthritis and the resulting reconstructions portrayed Neanderthal man as a hairy, slouching, bent-kneed, dim-witted subhuman who it seemed desirable to banish at once from the human family tree. Later re-examination of the skeleton revealed how inaccurate these reconstructions were but by then the damage was done and the image has stuck in the popular consciousness. By the 1950s scientific opinion was beginning to regard Neanderthal man as an intelligent and social creature who was a possible ancestor of modern Europeans: it became fashionable to emphasize his humanness as much as possible and Neanderthal man achieved the status of a sub-species of modern man – *Homo sapiens neanderthalensis*. In the last few years, however, there has been a reaction against this view and, though he is now re-garded as "differently human" rather than subhuman, Neanderthal man has once again been relegated (in the nicest possible way) to an evolutionary dead end.

There are certainly important physical differences between Neanderthals and modern humans but the crux of the problem is, are these significant enough to make Neanderthal man a separate species? After all, there are significant physical differences between a Chihuahua and a Great Dane but they are both still the same species. The controversy of Neanderthal man's place in human evolution could be settled once and for all if Neanderthal DNA could be recovered and compared with that of modern humans, but attempts to extract DNA from fossilized Neanderthal bones have so far failed. What is really needed is a frozen Neanderthal corpse; perhaps one will be disgorged by a melting glacier as a result of global warming?

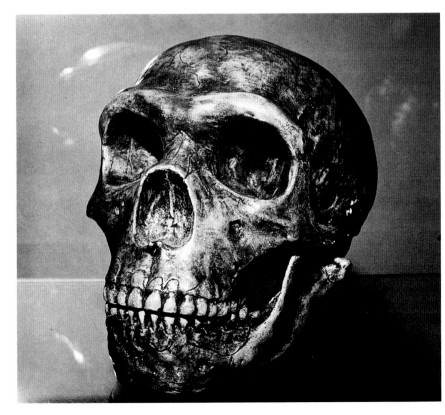

Below: Reconstruction of the skull of a Neanderthal man. Though having a larger brain than modern humans, Neanderthal man retained the low-vaulted cranium and brow ridges typical of *Homo erectus*. The face and nose were much larger than a modern human's and the jaw was more prognathous.

The present consensus is that Neanderthal man began to evolve out of European or Near Eastern "archaic *Homo sapiens*" about 230,000 years ago and reached his full development by about 150,000 years ago. There were several important differences between Neanderthals and modern humans. Neanderthal man's skull still possessed the prominent brow ridges which were also a feature of the *Homo erectus* skull, his face was large, with a broad, long nose, receding chin and protruding jaws, which had plenty of room for his large teeth – Neanderthal man did not have any problems with wisdom teeth. Neanderthal man was low-browed and his cranial vault was long and low. His brain however was exceptionally large – up to 20 percent larger than a modern human's. This does not mean that Neanderthal man was more intelligent than modern man but is simply a consequence of his greater bulk as there is a tendency among modern humans for larger people to have larger brains: to some extent the brain grows to fill the space available for it and, as we all know, the biggest people are not necessarily the smartest. Neanderthal man had a longer tongue than

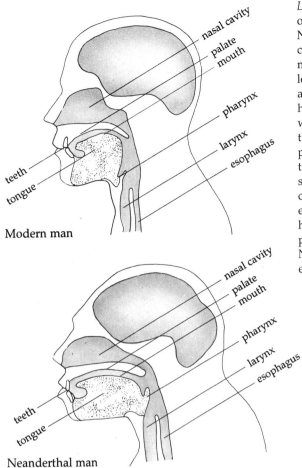

Modern man

Neanderthal man

Left: The vocal apparatus of a modern human and Neanderthal man compared. Neanderthal man had a larger and less mobile tongue than a modern human and his larynx (voice box) was positioned higher in the throat. Thus he was probably unable to make the same range of sounds, and so talk and communicate as effectively, as a modern human. This may have played a role in Neanderthal man's extinction.

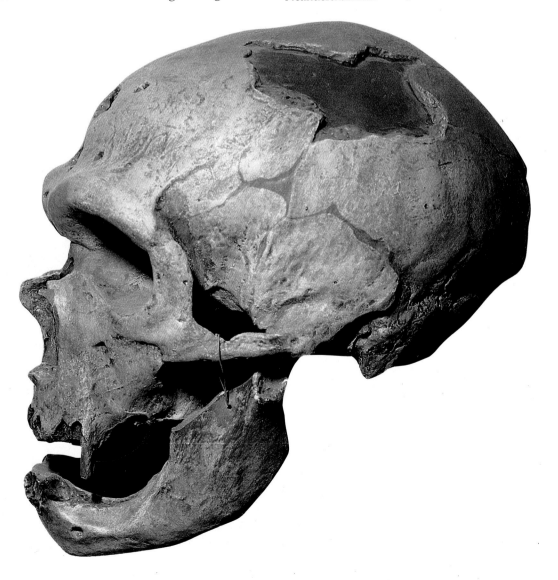

Left: The skull of the so-called "Old man of La Chapelle-aux-Saints." Discovered in 1908, this was one of the first complete skeletons of Neanderthal man to be found. The old man was crippled with arthritis and could not have fended for himself; other members of the Neanderthal band must have taken care of him.

Left: Partial skeleton of a male Neanderthal from Kebana, Israel, *c.* 60,000 years old. Though physically adapted to cold, Neanderthal populations moved out of Europe into the milder Near East at the height of the last glaciation.

Right and below: An early twentieth-century reconstruction of Neanderthal man (*right*) as a slouching dim-wit gnawing a raw bone. This image of the Neanderthals lives on in the popular consciousness, but the reconstruction of an alert and intelligent Neanderthal female (*below*) is more in keeping with modern scientific opinion.

modern humans and a voice box which was positioned far closer to the base of the skull than a modern human's. It is thought that these differences meant that Neanderthal man could not produce as wide a range of sounds as modern humans and would have had to speak more slowly, limiting his ability to communicate verbally.

Neanderthal man was a little shorter and somewhat broader on average than modern humans, with relatively short legs. The proportions of the limbs differed from modern humans in that the forearms and lower legs of Neanderthal man were relatively shorter, and the upper arms and legs relatively longer than ours. However, he walked with a normal upright gait, just like modern humans. The muscle attachments on Neanderthal bones were very large, indicating that he was powerfully muscled and probably twice as strong as an average modern human. Despite these anatomical differences, if he were washed, shaved, given a haircut and a suit of clothes, Neanderthal man would probably not attract much attention to himself if he came walking down the street today. Neanderthals grew up quickly and aged fast compared to modern humans.

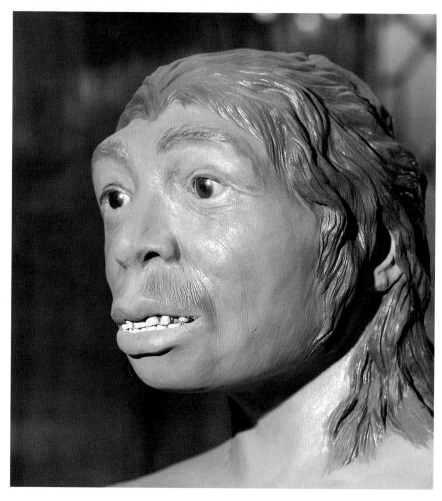

Neanderthal children were considerably more advanced than modern children of comparable age while only 10 percent of Neanderthals appear to have lived beyond the age of 35 compared to 50 percent of modern hunter-gatherers.

There is widespread agreement that Neanderthal man's distinctive physique was the result of evolutionary adaptations to living in a cold climate. The period of Neanderthal man's evolution was one of transition from a mild interglacial to a cold glacial period which would have created strong selective pressures among northern populations of early humans in favor of characteristics which increased resistance to cold. The proportions of Neanderthal man's body and limbs are similar, though more pronounced, to those found in modern humans, like the Eskimo and the Lapps, who live in arctic environments: the short stocky build and the relatively short forelimbs help to reduce heat loss from the body. Conversely, modern human populations of hot desert areas, such as Arizona Indians or Kalahari Bushmen, have a lighter build and longer forelimbs which aid heat loss. Though it has no parallel in modern populations, Neanderthal man's big nose is thought to have helped warm cold air before it reached the lungs and so reduce heat loss through breathing. Their large bodies might have helped the Neanderthals build up large reserves of fat to help see them through the long Ice Age winters. Modern depictions of Neanderthal man show him with rather more body hair than is normal today. Though this might be a likely adaptation to a cold climate, such depictions have more to do with the artist's preconceptions about what constitutes primitiveness than with fact: we actually have no idea how much body hair Neanderthal man had, if any.

Neanderthal man occupied a range that extended from Wales in the northwest and Spain in the southwest right across central and southern Europe, through the Near East and Iran to the foothills of the Hindu Kush mountains in central Asia. The early Neanderthals favored sheltered valleys in rolling hill country, such as the Dordogne region of France, southern Germany, and central Europe. During glacial periods the uplands were open steppe grasslands rich in game, such as reindeer, red deer, aurochs (wild cattle), musk ox, ibex, horse, woolly rhinoceros, and mammoth. The valleys had thin pinewoods, essential for firewood, and caves for shelter. By about 60,000 years ago

the Neanderthals had successfully adapted to life on the open plains and higher mountains and were able to spread into the windswept but game-filled Russian and central Asian steppes.

The Neanderthals preferred to hunt smaller herd animals such as red deer, reindeer, horse, and aurochs. Mammoth and woolly rhino also featured in the Neanderthal diet but, as hunting such large animals would have been very dangerous, it is likely that most of this meat was scavenged from carcasses. However, there is evidence from the Channel Islands (then joined to France because of the low sea level) that they also stampeded big-game animals over cliffs to their deaths. Many Neanderthal skeletons show evidence of injuries, suggesting that they killed many animals at close quarters. The Neanderthals' powerful build shows that they led physically demanding lives and it is possible that they pursued prey on foot over long distances, perhaps even running them down. In order to survive the winters, the Neanderthals would have needed to store meat but the freezing con-

ditions would have made that easy. Each group would have needed a hunting territory of several hundred square miles so the Neanderthal population was probably very dispersed: there may never have been more than a few thousand Neanderthals in the whole of Europe. Though meat must have formed the main part of their diet, Neanderthals did collect berries and probably knew of the medicinal properties of some plants.

Neanderthal man is closely associated with a new toolmaking tradition known as the Mousterian (after a major Neanderthal site at Le Moustier in France). Neanderthal man still made handaxes but he was a much more skilled toolmaker than *Homo erectus* and archaic *Homo sapiens* had been. Neanderthal toolmakers did not just pick up a suitably shaped rock and start banging away at it as earlier toolmakers had done. By carefully pre-shaping the rock into a disk, Neanderthal toolmakers were able to strike off far more usable flakes than had been possible using the older techniques. Compared to the Acheulean technique of *Homo erectus*, Neanderthal man was able to extract up to eight

Above: Neanderthals hunted mammoth by stampeding them over cliffs or into bogs where they could be killed more easily. On the whole, however, Neanderthals preferred smaller game such as deer which could be hunted with less physical danger. Many mammoths, such as this one discovered in the nineteenth century, have been found perfectly preserved in permafrost in Siberia.

Left: Neanderthal man could manufacture a wider range of tools than any earlier hominid: heavy projectile points for hunting large game (*left*); side-scrapers used in butchery and for cleaning hides before they were made into clothing (*center*); and disk flakes used as multi-purpose tools (*right*).

times as much cutting edge from the same weight of rock, saving him a great deal of time finding and carrying suitable toolmaking materials. Some Neanderthals learned how to haft stone blades to the end of poles to make more effective spears than had been available to *Homo erectus*. In some areas, such as Israel about 90,000 years ago, the Mousterian toolmaking technique was also used by anatomically modern humans. The development of flake tools by Neanderthal man and other archaic humans is the main technological development of the Middle Paleolithic, 150,000-40,000 BP (Before Present).

Cold adapted as he was, in order to survive on the bleak plains of Ice Age Europe, Neanderthal man must have been able to make clothing for himself. As no needles or other sewing tools have been found, these clothes must have been simple in design. No body ornaments have been found but red ocher has been found at some Neanderthal

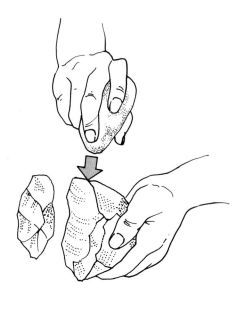

Mousterian

Left: With the Mousterian toolmaking technique used by the Neanderthals, disk-shaped flakes were struck off a carefully prepared stone core. These flakes were versatile and could be made into a variety of tools. The Mousterian technique also allowed more efficient use of stone than earlier methods.

sites; perhaps they used it to decorate their bodies as many later humans have done? The Neanderthals often lived in caves and probably built windbreaks across the entrances to make them more comfortable. Out on the plains they built huts like one which has been excavated at Molodova in the Ukraine which had foundations built of mammoth bones. The Neanderthals were more skillful in their management of fire than *Homo erectus* had been and they had learned how to make hearths to burn wood more efficiently.

Little is known about the structure of Neanderthal society but their groups were probably strongly cohesive. The skeleton of an old crippled man from a cave at Shanidar in Iraq shows that Neanderthals did care for elderly or disabled group members. Tooth wear analysis shows that the old cripple paid for his keep by chewing hides, probably to soften them before making them into clothes. Neanderthals seem to have had some sense of awareness of themselves as being distinct from other animals and may even have had some kind of religious beliefs.

They were the first humans deliberately to bury their dead (this is one reason why we have more skeletal remains for Neanderthal man than for any earlier hominid). One Neanderthal at the cave at Shanidar was laid to rest on a bed of spring flowers, some of which are known to have medicinal properties. A burial of a nine-year-old Neanderthal boy at Teshnik-Tash in Uzbekistan was protected by a cage made of pairs of goat horns which perhaps had some symbolic or ritual significance. Neanderthals may not have been ancestors of ours but they do seem to have been on the way to developing thoughts and feelings which we moderns can recognize.

Neanderthal man became extinct about 28,000 years ago. There are many theories about why this happened but nearly all of them agree that it had something to do with the arrival of anatomically modern humans in Europe about 40,000 years ago. If the genetic differences between Neanderthal man and modern humans were small enough, interbreeding would have been possible and the Neanderthals could simply have been absorbed by the newcomers. If so, Neanderthal man is not really extinct, as many of his genes will still survive in modern humans of European ancestry. If, on the other hand, as many anthropologists believe, Neanderthal man was a completely separate species of human, interbreeding would not have been possible and we are forced to conclude that our ancestors drove the Neanderthals to extinction. The Neanderthals lived side by side with the newcomers for around 12,000 years before becoming extinct, so it is unlikely that they were the victims of a campaign of genocide (though the behavior of twentieth-century Europeans shows that it was not impossible). There must have been at least some peaceful contacts between the two groups, as some Neanderthals adopted new toolmaking techniques from the moderns.

The most likely scenario is that the newcomers progressively outcompeted the Neanderthals. At first, the cold-adapted Neanderthals had Europe to themselves, but around 40,000 years ago anatomically modern humans in the Near East developed the abilities to adapt to the frigid environment of Europe through cultural innovation. They could sew, so they could make warmer clothes and though they were puny by Neanderthal standards their hunting technology was far superior. Probably, the newcomers, known as Cro-Magnons from a site in France, could communicate better than the Neanderthals, so their hunting bands co-operated more effectively, and as they lived longer, skills and knowledge were passed on more effectively through the generations. Whichever scenario – absorption or replacement – is true, the Neanderthals were in decline by 35,000 years ago: the last groups held out in Spain until about 28,000 years ago.

What then is the significance of Neanderthal man for the history of the human race? If anything Neanderthal man shows us just how chancy our evolution was. Had the last glacial been a few degrees colder, then perhaps it might have been "modern" man that lost out in competition to the cold-adapted Neanderthals and became an evolutionary dead end. Neanderthal man represents just one of the possible roads that human evolution might have taken, that is by adapting physically to different climates and habitats. As it was, the Neanderthals lost out to a different kind of human, one that adapted to different environments entirely by cultural and technological means.

Below: A large flake tool found in a Neanderthal burial at Tabun, Israel, *c.*60,000 years old.

CHAPTER FIVE

All About Eve: DNA and the Origins of Modern Man

While archaic *Homo sapiens* in Europe was evolving into Neanderthal man, archaic *Homo sapiens* in Africa was evolving into anatomically modern *Homo sapiens*. This evolution was complete by about 135,000 years ago. By about 90,000 years ago anatomically modern humans had appeared in the Near East, by 50,000 years ago they had appeared in East Asia and by 40,000 years ago they were in Europe and Australia. These are the bald facts: their interpretation is the most hotly contested battlefield in the whole field of paleoanthropology (a discipline dominated by big egos).

There are two rival models of the origins of modern humans: the multiregional and the single origin or "Out of Africa" models. The Out of Africa model maintains that modern humans evolved in Africa from African *Homo erectus* via African archaic *Homo sapiens*. Then about 100,000 years ago modern humans began to spread out of Africa into Eurasia replacing the resident populations of Neanderthals and Asian *Homo erectus*/archaic *Homo sapiens* which became extinct. The multiregional model rejects this view and maintains that there was evolutionary continuity in several regions of the world – Africa, Europe, East, and Southeast Asia – leading local populations of *Homo erectus* independently to evolve through archaic *Homo sapiens* into modern humans. Thus *Homo erectus* in Europe evolved into archaic *Homo sapiens*, then into Neanderthal man and then into modern man. Similar processes took place among local *Homo erectus* populations in Africa and Asia. If the multiregional model is correct then the different human races are of very long standing and their origins could go back as far as the first diaspora of *Homo erectus* out of Africa a million years ago. If the Out of Africa model is correct then the human races have arisen only in the last 90,000-40,000 years. Unfortunately the implications of these rival theories

have not been lost on either racists or anti-racists and there is a danger that the debate could become politicized.

Critics of the multiregional model point out that it is fantastically improbable that isolated groups of hominids living in widely differing habitats should all evolve exactly in parallel and reach exactly the same level of physical and mental development at exactly the same time. It has not happened anywhere else in the natural world. Partisans for multiregionalism, however, point out that the hominids probably did not form completely isolated breeding populations. For example African archaic *Homo sapiens* at the edge of his range was able occasionally to interbreed with European archaic *Homo sapiens* at the edge of his. Over the hundreds of thousands of years of human evolution there was probably enough exchange of genes between the different populations to

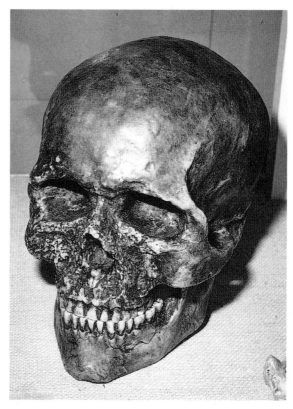

Left: Skull of Cro-Magnon man, around 25,000 years old. Cro-Magnon man, named after the site where the skull was discovered, was one of the earliest anatomically modern human inhabitants of Europe.

Right: Anatomically modern humans discovered how to make use of stone by striking long thin blades from a prepared core by indirect pressure. At around 100,000 years old, this blade and blade core from Klasies River Mouth Cave, South Africa, are among the oldest artifacts yet known which can be ascribed to anatomically modern humans.

prevent them becoming entirely separate species and to keep their evolutionary development in step so that all the populations arrived at the same point at around the same time.

In 1987 the debate seemed to have been finally settled in favor of a single origin for all modern humans with the publication of DNA sequencing research which suggested that we all share a common female ancestor who lived in Africa between 285,000 and 143,000 years ago. The basis of this research was a comparison of the mitochondrial DNA (mtDNA) of widely separated human populations and, inevitably, this common ancestor was quickly dubbed "Mitochondrial Eve." What then is this mtDNA which can seemingly tell us so much about our ancestry?

DNA is the complex self-replicating molecule that carries a cell's genetic material. Most of a cell's DNA is found in the nucleus but a smaller amount is found in thread-like membranes called mitochondria in the body of the cell outside the nucleus. MtDNA can be inherited only from the mother as the father's sperm cannot carry mtDNA (a sperm is a highly specialized cell which consists only of a nucleus and so does not contain mitochondria). Nuclear DNA is inherited from both parents and so is subject to potentially infinite recombinations: mtDNA, being inherited only from the mother is not subject to recombination and so is passed on from mother to child through the generations unchanged except for random mutations. This makes it possible to use mtDNA to trace ancestry through the female line.

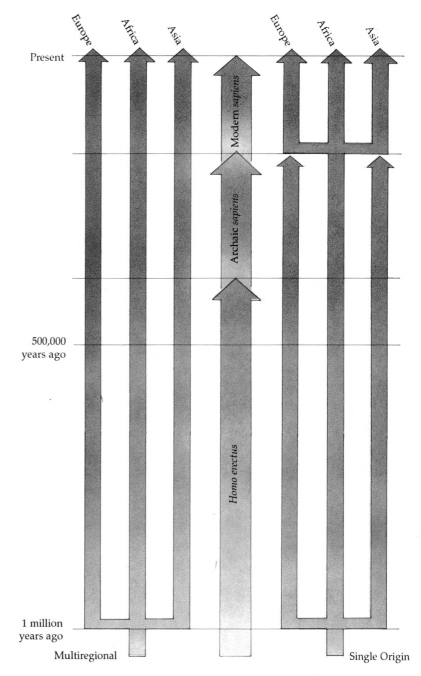

Above: The rival theories of the evolution of anatomically modern man. The multiregionalists (*left*) claim that modern humans evolved simultaneously in Africa, Europe, and Asia from the local *Homo erectus* populations. The single origin theory (*right*) claims instead that modern humans evolved only in Africa and then spread to other parts of the world, replacing the local *Homo erectus* populations.

MtDNA mutates at an average rate of 2-4 percent per million years. By comparing the differences between the mtDNA of different individuals (or different species) it is possible to calculate the length of time that has elapsed since they shared a common ancestor. For instance, if there was a difference of 0.1 percent between the mtDNA of two people we ought to be able to say that they shared a common ancestor 50,000-100,000 years ago. By comparing the mtDNA of different human populations, researchers discovered that the differences between the mtDNA of people of African descent was twice as great as the differences between the mtDNA of people from the rest of the world. Modern Europeans are apparently more closely related to South American Indians than are western Africans to southern Africans. The best explanation of this seemed to be as follows. About 200,000 years ago an African woman passed on her mtDNA to her female children, and as they in turn had female children her mtDNA became more and more widely spread. With the passing of the generations, random mutations took place in the mtDNA, gradually widening the differences between "Eve's" descendants. Then, about 100,000 years ago a small group of Eve's descendants, all of them closely related and so sharing similar mtDNA, left Africa and eventually their descendants spread throughout the rest of the world. Thus Eve's African descendants have had 200,000 years of mtDNA mutations since sharing a common ancestor, while the people of the rest of the world have had only half as long. This would account for the greater genetic diversity of African populations as well as the relative lack of genetic variation in the rest of the world's population.

In reality, however, things are not quite so simple. Firstly, Mitochondrial Eve is not our only ancestor, she is only our common ancestor for mtDNA: most of our DNA is nuclear DNA which we have inherited from an unknown number of both male and female ancestors. Female ancestors who had only male children would have been prevented from contributing their mtDNA to any future generations: probably, Eve's is the only mtDNA to survive because she and her female descendants were far more successful in having female children than their

Klasies River Mouth Cave has the earliest evidence of humans exploiting marine food sources. Shellfish, penguins, and cape fur seals (*above*) were collected and caught in large numbers and whale carcasses were scavenged.

Above right: Upper Paleolithic tools from southwestern France, *c.* 25,000 years old. End-scrapers (*left and center*) – a typical tool made from a blade – and (*right*) a simple scraper made from a rough stone. Scrapers were used to clean hides prior to making them into clothes or tents.

Left: Obsidian blades from the island of Melos, Greece *c.*8000 BC. By the end of the Ice Age short sea voyages were being made from the Greek mainland to Melos to collect obsidian, a volcanic glass which makes excellent tools. Good toolmaking stone could be traded over long distances by Upper Paleolithic man.

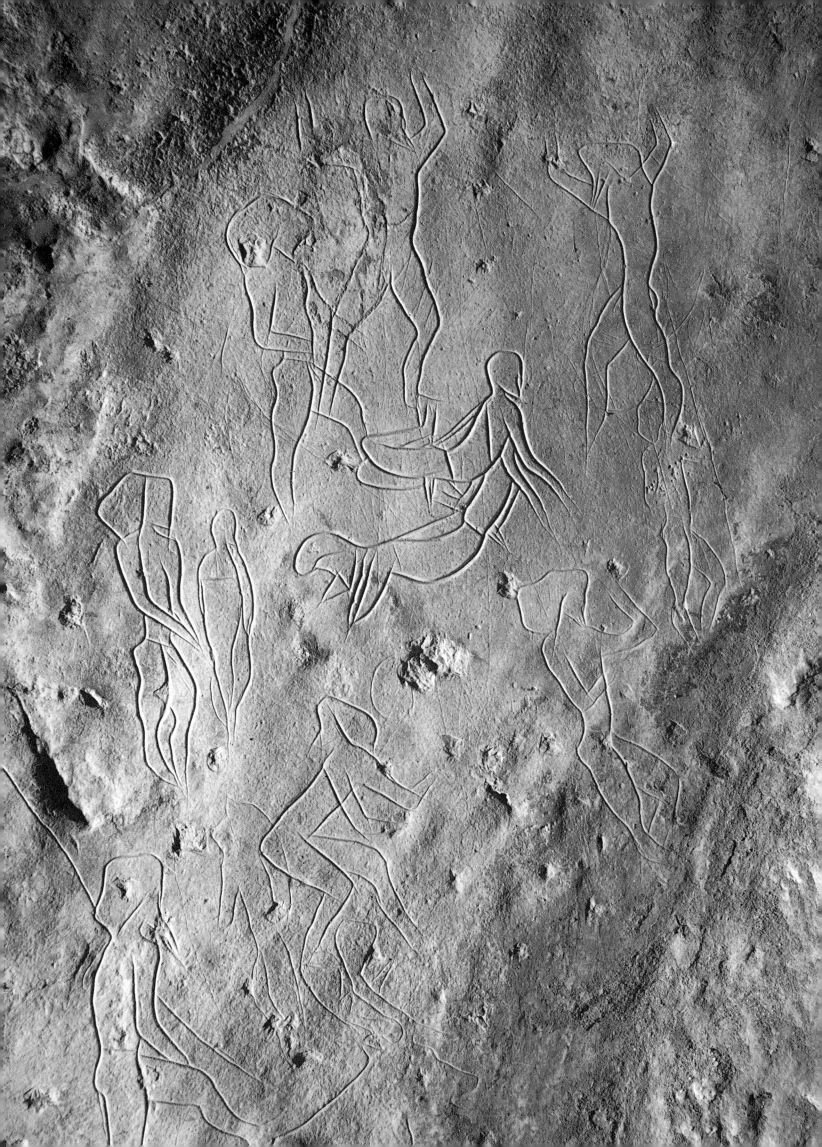

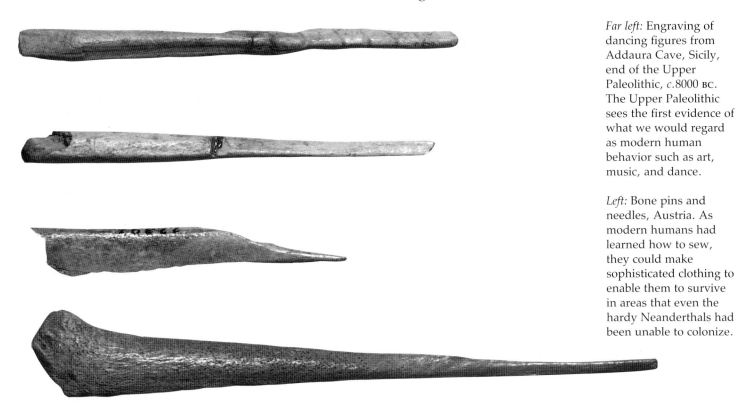

Far left: Engraving of dancing figures from Addaura Cave, Sicily, end of the Upper Paleolithic, *c.*8000 BC. The Upper Paleolithic sees the first evidence of what we would regard as modern human behavior such as art, music, and dance.

Left: Bone pins and needles, Austria. As modern humans had learned how to sew, they could make sophisticated clothing to enable them to survive in areas that even the hardy Neanderthals had been unable to colonize.

contemporaries. This raises a small question mark over the Out of Africa model. Mitochondrial Eve might have lived in Africa but that does not necessarily mean that all of our ancestors did.

A potentially greater problem concerns the average rate of mutation in mtDNA. All averages are subject to variability and the smaller the sample the greater the potential for variation. (Try tossing a coin six times: there might very easily be six heads or no heads at all, a 100 percent variation either way from the theoretical average. Then toss the coin 100 times, the result will be very close to 50 heads and 50 tails.) Therefore, unlike many dating methods, DNA sequencing becomes more accurate the longer the time period concerned. There may be little room for doubt that the human and chimpanzee lineages divided about 6 million years ago but how sure can we be that over a period as short as 200,000 or 100,000 years the mutation rate of mtDNA has remained within the 2-4 percent norm in all of the world's peoples all of the time? When this potential for variability is taken into account, critics of the Out of Africa model claim that Eve might have lived as recently as 60,000 years ago or as long as 1 million, about the time that *Homo erectus* moved out of Africa. If the latter date was true, the multiregionalists could, after all, be right.

Research has now moved on to the far more complex task of assessing variability in nuclear DNA. This work indicates a primary African/non-African split in the human population and a subsequent split into two major groups: one comprising Europeans, Middle Eastern peoples, Indians, Northeast Asians, and Amerindians; the other Southeast Asians, Pacific islanders, Australians, and New Guineans. It is believed that variation in nuclear DNA accumulates at a constant rate (though this is as yet not proven beyond question), thus the amount of genetic variation found in modern populations can be used to calculate the time at which the ancestral population lived. Recent estimates suggest that the variation found in modern human populations has taken about 150,000 years to develop and that the African/non-African split took place about 100,000 years ago. These dates tie in very well with the evidence from mtDNA but have the same limitations. Nevertheless two separate techniques now point to broadly the same conclusion: that all modern humans are descended from a single ancestral population that lived in Africa between 200,000 and 100,000 years ago.

Archeological evidence also tends to favor a single origin for modern humans in Africa. Archaic forms of *Homo sapiens* begin to appear in Africa about 500,000 years ago, about 200,000 years earlier than happens elsewhere and it is in Africa that anatomically modern *Homo sapiens* first appears around 135,000 years ago. Nor is there evidence from elsewhere in the world of other regional populations making the same

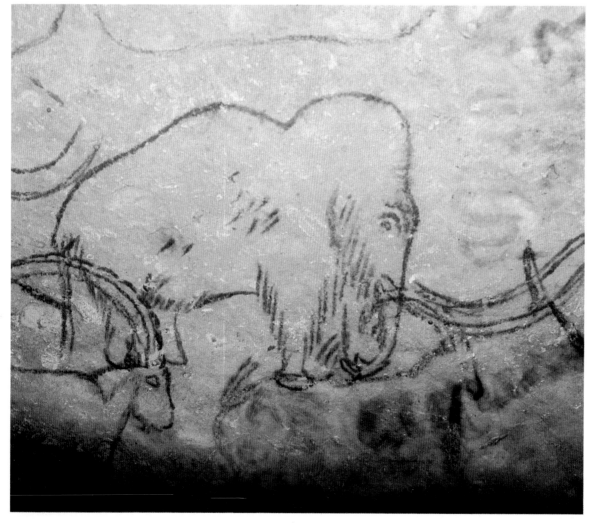

Above and left: The cave art of southwestern France and northern Spain is possibly the most spectacular evidence that Upper Paleolithic man was mentally as well as physically fully modern. This engraving of a reindeer from La Madeleine, Dordogne, France (*above*), and a drawing of a mammoth and ibexes from Rouffignac, Dordogne (*left*), are both *c.* 20,000-14,000 years old. The purpose and meaning of these haunting images is unknown.

Far right: Female head with a plaited or braided hairstyle from Brassempouy, France, *c.* 25,000 years old. The obvious concern Upper Paleolithic humans showed for their appearance is a sign of their developed sense of self-awareness.

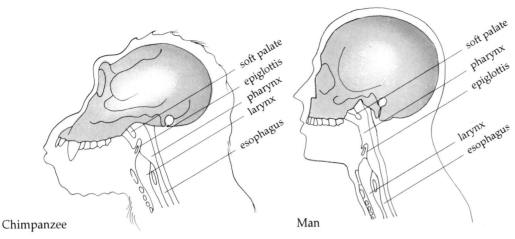

Chimpanzee   Man

Left: The position of the anatomically modern human's larynx low down in the throat enables them to make a far wider and precise range of sounds than any ape (*left*) or earlier human such as Neanderthal man (see page 35). The ability to communicate effectively and to talk to one's self was a major factor in the evolution of self-awareness.

gradual transition from archaic to modern forms. In Europe the Neanderthal and anatomically modern Cro-Magnon populations were clearly distinct: the former did not evolve into the latter but was replaced by them. In China primitive forms of archaic *Homo sapiens* are known up to about 100,000 years ago, then there is a gap in the fossil record. The earliest anatomically modern human remains date to 25,000 years ago and there is no evidence of any transitional forms. In fact these earliest modern human inhabitants of China were anatomically similar to the Cro-Magnons of Europe, suggesting that the distinctive Mongoloid features of East Asians have evolved only in the last 25,000 years. In Southeast Asia advanced forms of *Homo erectus* survived until 60,000 years ago when they were replaced by anatomically modern humans, again, without there being any evidence of transitional forms.

It does look very much as if anatomically modern humans did evolve only in Africa and then spread out across the world replacing the local archaic and *Homo erectus* populations. The genetic evidence is not conclusive enough to rule out the possibility that the moderns may sometimes have interbred with the archaics as they colonized new areas and that, therefore, some of their genes could have entered the modern gene pool, but this is not the same thing as multiregional evolution.

What characteristics did the early moderns have that enabled them to replace all of the world's other human populations? Technology is not the answer, for millennia the tools used by the moderns were no more advanced than those used by the archaics. The high forehead and high-vaulted cranium of modern man may or may not indicate a different brain structure to earlier hominids and as the moderns actually had smaller brains than some of the archaics like Neanderthal man, there are no obvious

Left: An important sign of the evolution of self-awareness is the appearance of body ornaments, like this Upper Paleolithic necklace.

Right: Statuettes of a dancing girl from Tursac, southwestern France, *c.* 25,000 years old. Though the meaning and purpose of the statuettes are unknown, they seem to be expressive of joy and delight in life.

answers here either. However, early modern humans were anatomically much less robust than any earlier humans, indicating that they had evolved a way of life that was physically less demanding than that of the Neanderthals and the archaics. Unfortunately, we can only speculate about what caused this change in behavior. The most plausible explanation at present is that the voice box and tongue of anatomically modern humans enabled them to speak fluently. Thus, fluent speech allowed the moderns to pass on information and ideas more effectively and to co-operate more closely in complex tasks such as hunting or self-defense. Initially this probably gave the moderns a small advantage over the archaics, but fluent speech also caused the moderns to change the way they thought.

Fluent speech led eventually to the development of language which enabled the moderns not only to articulate and communicate their thoughts to others, it also allowed them to listen to their own thoughts, in other words, to talk to themselves and so to become truly self-aware with everything that that implies. This was a very gradual process but there can be no doubt about when it was completed. Quite suddenly 50,000-40,000 years ago we find the first evidence of art and symbolic thought, body ornaments, musical instruments, complex religious beliefs and rituals, and of an increasing pace of technological development. These developments mark the end of humanity's long physical and mental evolution: fully modern man had arrived.

CHAPTER SIX

The Long Walk: The Peopling of the Earth

When European seafarers began to explore the world in the sixteenth century they found people almost everywhere. The only large landmass that was uninhabited was Antarctica and even modern technology can do no more than sustain a few scientific bases there at great cost. A few islands in the Arctic, Atlantic, Indian, and Pacific oceans were still uninhabited but that was all. With few exceptions, the peoples discovered by the modern European explorers on their travels had been settled in their homelands for so long that neither their myths nor their historical traditions could shed light on their origins. Fortunately, the earth has preserved much of what memory had forgotten and it is now possible to reconstruct the story of the human colonization of the world in some detail.

The range of the earliest hominids – the australopithecines and *Homo habilis* – had been limited to the broad savannah belt which stretches from Ethiopia through East Africa to the Transvaal in South Africa. *Homo erectus* spread over a much wider area but he too remained confined to environments which were similar to the African savannah where he had evolved. The Neanderthals in western Eurasia successfully adapted to life in a far colder environment than any earlier hominid but it was anatomically modern *Homo sapiens* who finally broke free of environmental constraints and colonized the whole globe. However, just like *Homo*

Above right: Family tree of the modern human races based on a comparison of their DNA. The results suggest that the humans who left Africa divided into two populations, a northern one which gave rise to the Caucasians, Northeast Asians, and Amerindians, and a southern one from which the Southeast Asians, Polynesians, and Australian Aborigines descended.

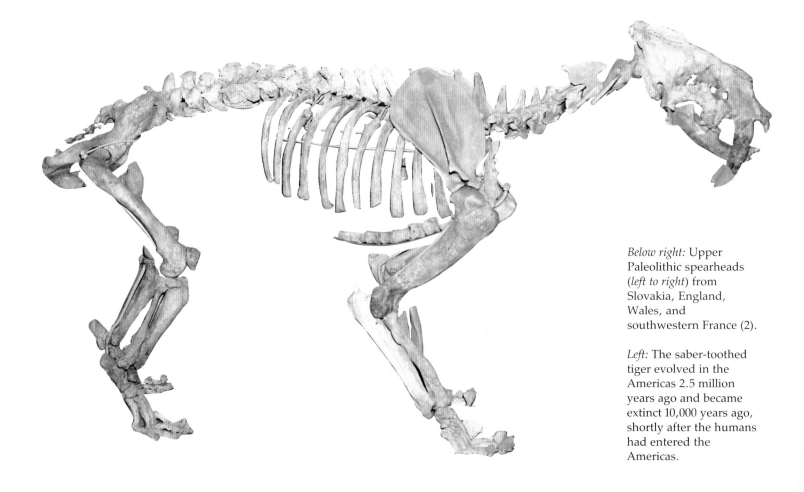

Below right: Upper Paleolithic spearheads (*left to right*) from Slovakia, England, Wales, and southwestern France (2).

Left: The saber-toothed tiger evolved in the Americas 2.5 million years ago and became extinct 10,000 years ago, shortly after the humans had entered the Americas.

erectus, modern *Homo sapiens* evolved on the East African savannah and he naturally had a preference for similar types of environment.

Modern humans had fully colonized the savannahs of Africa by 100,000 BP (Before Present) and had effectively run out of space. The arid lands of southwestern Africa remained uncolonized until about 27,000 years ago, while humans did not move into the West African rainforests until as late as 6500 BP. Tropical rainforests are the most productive environments on Earth in terms of biomass: why then did it take so long for humans to colonize them? Unfortunately for humans, most of the biomass is made up of inedible wood. Forest animals tend to be smaller than grassland animals and they form smaller herds and are much harder to find. There are plenty of vegetable foods, like nuts and fruits, in the forest but these are concentrated in the treetops a couple of hundred feet above the ground. This would have been no problem for our primate ancestors but our evolution has unfitted us for life in the trees. Having adapted to life on the ground, there was no going back to the forest. The rainforests were only opened up to human colonization by the adoption of agriculture. By cutting a clearing in the forest and planting carbohydrate-rich vegetables like yams, humans could at last harness the tremendous productive powers of the rainforest environment. Some modern

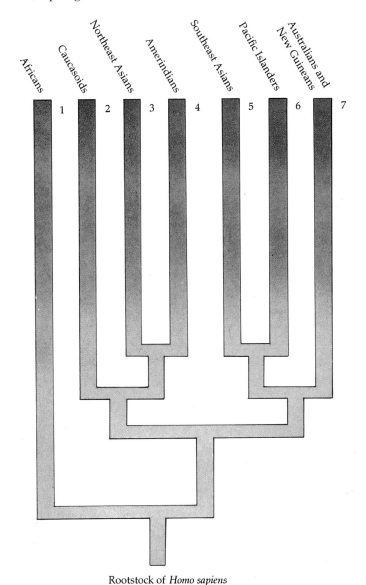

Rootstock of *Homo sapiens*

rainforest peoples, such as the pygmies, have adapted to a hunter-gatherer way of life but they are not actually self-sufficient and must trade forest products with neighboring farmers for some of their food.

The Sahara desert was the main obstacle to humans spreading out of Africa but there have been periods of higher rainfall when the desert gave way to grasslands. It was probably in one such period around 100,000 years ago that a small number of closely related humans (perhaps a single hunter-gatherer band) began to move north out of Africa. By 90,000 BP their descendants were living in caves like Skhul and Qafzeh in Israel in close proximity to Neanderthals. From here it was only a short step into Europe but it was one that humans did not take for another 50,000 years. By 90,000 BP the climate was deteriorating and the advancing ice sheets were forcing even some of the hardy Neanderthals to move south: human technology and social organization was not yet up to such a challenging environment. Expansion continued eastward across the dry grasslands of the Middle East into India and Southeast Asia by around 60,000 years ago.

So much of the world's water was locked up in ice sheets during the last glaciation that sea levels fell by over 400 feet. In Southeast Asia this caused the shallow continental shelf to become dry land: the islands of the Indonesian archipelago became mountain ranges in an extensive plain covered with grasslands, open forest, and patches of rainforest. As in Africa humans shunned the rainforest, preferring more open country. Again it was only the adoption of agriculture 10,000-5000 years ago that permitted extensive human settlement in these areas. The Southeast Asian peoples made one of the great technological breakthroughs of human history – they learned how to make seaworthy boats. No remains of these pioneering seafarers' boats have been found (the post-glacial rise in sea levels will have submerged any evidence long ago) but they probably used rafts or large dug-out canoes. Whatever these boats were like, they enabled people to make coastal voyages, go sea fishing, and colonize offshore islands. Possibly they went on voyages of exploration, deliberately seeking new lands to colonize; sometimes fishermen may have got blown out to sea and sighted new lands by accident. However it happened, sometime between 60,000 and 40,000 BP people from Southeast Asia began to colonize Australia and New Guinea.

Above: The main human migration from Northeast Asia into the Americas took place *c.* 11,500 years ago when retreating ice sheets opened a land route from Alaska to the Great Plains. Other immigrants may have avoided the ice sheets by sailing down the Pacific coast in hide boats similar to this modern Eskimo umiak.

Right: The first seafarers were the ancestors of the Australian Aborigines who crossed the Timor Sea from Southeast Asia over 40,000 years ago. Their boats have not survived but they were probably simple rafts or dug-out canoes like these modern examples in the Okovango Delta, Botswana.

Left: The Jones-Miller Paleo-Indian bison kill site in Colorado, *c.* 10,000 years old. Several hundred animals were killed here, probably after they were driven into a specially constructed corral. The Paleo-Indians often used highly wasteful hunting methods, killing far more bison that they could use by stampeding whole herds over cliffs or into narrow arroyos, where they would be crushed to death.

Right: Prehistoric aboriginal cave-wall painting of a kangaroo. The first humans to reach Australia found a fauna which was quite different from anything they had encountered before.

Following pages: Reconstruction of a sturdy hut built of mammoth bones, Mezhirich, Ukraine, *c.* 20,000 years old. The bone framework would have been covered with hides to make it weatherproof. Despite the intense cold and lack of shelter, the Ice Age steppes of eastern Europe were an attractive environment for a resourceful hunting people because of their plentiful game.

Because of the low sea levels, Australia, Tasmania, and New Guinea were at this time a single massive island, now known as Sahul. Australia was separated from the Southeast Asian island of Timor by only 40 miles (65km) of open sea: New Guinea was only slightly further away from Sulawesi. The voyage need not have been a difficult one, but it is remarkable that it happened at all at such an early date (there are no archeological remains of boats older than about 8000 years). The native peoples of modern Australasia show great physical diversity and it is likely that there were several further waves of migrants from Asia after the initial colonists arrived. Some early Australian Aborigines showed strikingly archaic robustness. A 14,000-year-old skull from Kow Swamp in southern Australia shows signs of brow ridges and has a sloping forehead reminiscent of *Homo erectus* skulls. Multiregionalists have seized on this as evidence that there was some genetic mixing of the modern and *Homo erectus* populations of Southeast Asia before Sahul was colonized.

An alternative explanation is that some of the apparently archaic features of some Aboriginals were the result of deformation of the skull caused by head-binding in infancy, a custom practiced by some Aboriginal groups until recently.

Sahul had a marsupial fauna quite unlike anything humans had previously encountered and an enormous range of habitats from rainforests and upland grasslands in what is now New Guinea to glaciated mountains and tundra in Tasmania. Australia had an even lower rainfall than it does today but the cooler temperatures and resultant lower evaporation rates meant that there were many lakes in the interior, making it more favorable for human habitation than it is now. All of these habitats were colonized to some extent by about 30,000 BP, though population densities in forest and upland areas were very sparse until around 4000 years ago. The New Guineans and Aborigines adapted to forest life by using fire to thin the forests and stimulate new growth to attract game.

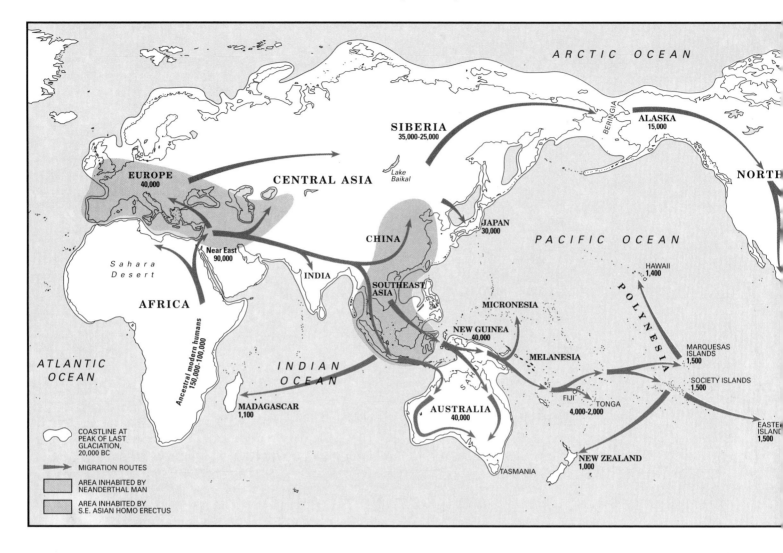

SIBERIA
35,000-25,000

BERINGIA

ALASKA
15,000

ARCTIC OCEAN

EUROPE
40,000

CENTRAL ASIA

Lake
Baikal

NORTH

Near East
90,000

CHINA

JAPAN
30,000

PACIFIC OCEAN

HAWAII
1,400

Sahara
Desert

INDIA

SOUTHEAST
ASIA

AFRICA

MICRONESIA

NEW GUINEA
40,000

P O L Y N E S I A

MARQUESAS
ISLANDS
1,500

ATLANTIC
OCEAN

Ancestral modern humans
150,000-100,000

MELANESIA

INDIAN
OCEAN

FIJI

TONGA
4,000-2,000

SOCIETY ISLANDS
1,500

MADAGASCAR
1,100

AUSTRALIA
40,000

EASTE
ISLAND
1,500

NEW ZEALAND
1,000

TASMANIA

COASTLINE AT
PEAK OF LAST
GLACIATION,
20,000 BC

MIGRATION ROUTES

AREA INHABITED BY
NEANDERTHAL MAN

AREA INHABITED BY
S.E. ASIAN HOMO ERECTUS

Above: The spread of
modern *Homo sapiens*
around the world.

Left: The first humans to
set foot in the Americas
followed herds of musk
oxen and other game
across the bleak tundras
of the Bering land-bridge
from Siberia to Alaska
toward the end of the
Ice Age.

Right: The first humans
to reach Alaska found
progress further south
blocked by glaciers and
ice sheets which
spanned the entire
continent from the
Pacific to the Atlantic.

New Guinea was the springboard for what is arguably the most remarkable of prehistoric man's achievements: the colonization of the Pacific. The first voyages of colonization took place around 32,000 years ago to New Britain and New Ireland, large islands which were within sight of the New Guinea mainland. By 20,000 BP the region had a well-established maritime economy in which cargoes of obsidian (a volcanic glass much prized by Stone Age toolmakers) were traded over distances of hundreds of miles. By 27,000 BP open sea voyages to the Solomon Islands, several days sailing from New Britain, were being made. However, beyond the Solomons the distances became much greater, the seas more dangerous and the islands much smaller and easier to miss. Moreover, the Pacific islands lacked any indigenous terrestrial mammals other than bats. Even if their boats were capable of making such long open sea voyages, there was nothing for hunter-gatherers to eat when they got there. These were obstacles that could not be overcome until the adoption of agriculture in New Guinea around 8000 years ago enabled colonizers to take food plants and domesticated animals with them and the development of the outrigger canoe 4000 years ago gave them an effective oceangoing craft. The colonization of Melanesia (the western Pacific islands) now followed quickly and by 3500 BP New Caledonia, Fiji, and Tonga had been settled. The settlement of Polynesia (the eastern Pacific islands) began from Tonga about 2000 years ago. By 1000 years ago even far-flung places like New Zealand, Easter Island, and Hawaii had been settled: by the time Europeans reached the Pacific in the sixteenth century, only a handful of islands remained uninhabited.

Only a little later than the first humans had reached Sahul, other humans – the Cro-Magnons – began to move north into the frozen plains of Europe and by 28,000 BP had completely displaced the Neanderthals. Herds of reindeer, horse, bison, and mammoth made the area attractive to hunters but conditions were harsh and, like the Neanderthals before them, the Cro-Magnons preferred to live in sheltered valleys in rolling uplands where caves and woodland could be found close to good hunting grounds. The remarkable achievements of these first modern Europeans are considered in the next chapter. Other groups moved out into the windswept steppes of eastern Europe, building huts of mammoth bones for shelter and burning fat-rich mammoth bones for

Left and below: The distinctive artifacts of the earlier Paleo-Indians are elegantly fluted spearheads. This spearhead (*left*) of the Clovis big-game hunting culture is *c.* 11,000 years old and this spearhead of the High Plains Folsom culture (*below*) is *c.* 9000 years old. Experiments have shown that these were among the most effective weapons made by Paleolithic man anywhere in the world.

fuel. By 35,000 years ago mammoth-hunting modern humans were established at Mal'ta near Lake Baikal in Siberia. These people had a rich artistic tradition which is comparable to that of the cave artists of western Europe but which probably originated locally. Modern humans were probably present in China by 35,000 BP and about 32,000 BP some made the short sea crossing to Japan. How these modern humans arrived in China is unknown, they could have come through central Asia and Mongolia, through Siberia or from Southeast Asia.

The tundras of northeastern Siberia were not settled until around 18,000 BP. The most important site in this region is Dyukhtai on the Aldan River, a couple of hundred miles inland from the Sea of Okhotsk. The Dyukhtai people hunted mammoth and musk-ox and had a distinctive method of making tiny "microblades" which links them with the inhabitants of northern China. Dyukhtai microblades are found all over northeastern Siberia by about 14,000 years ago, even north of the Arctic Circle. The most northerly site is at Berelekh, near the mouth of the Indigirka River, where the frozen remains of 140 mammoths, presumed drowned in spring floods, have been discovered. Dyukhtai microblades were found nearby among the remains of two mammoths and several dozen arctic hares. At the coldest point of the last glaciation, humans could live well by the Arctic Ocean but they could not yet sur-

vive in a rainforest: truly we are creatures of the Ice Age.

The last continents to be settled by humans were the Americas. No one seriously believes that the first Americans crossed the Atlantic in a Stone Age *Mayflower*, so they must have come from Northeast Asia. This conclusion is borne out by the fact that Amerindians and Northeast Asians both have similar distinctively shaped teeth, indicating a close relationship. Low sea

levels meant that for most of the period 100,000-12,000 BP it was possible to cross the Bering Sea between Siberia and Alaska without needing boats. Despite the intense cold, the area remained unglaciated and supported herds of mammoth, musk ox, and other herbivores. There was even a little scrubby woodland. Where there was food and fuel, there could also be people. The point of entry to the Americas must have been Alaska and so far there is no evidence of occupation there before about 15,000 BP. Settlement in Alaska much before 15,000 BP is, in any case, inherently unlikely since there were virtually no people in Northeast Asia until around 18,000 BP. Some early Alaskan sites have yielded microblade tools and it is probable that the first colonizers of the Americas were closely related to the Dyukhtai people.

For much of the last glaciation Alaska was cut off from the rest of the Americas by a massive ice sheet which stretched right across Canada from the Pacific coast ranges to the Atlantic and extended southward beyond the Great Lakes. After the glaciation had reached its peak 18,000 years ago, the Canadian ice sheet retreated and split into two smaller (but still huge) ice sheets, the Cordilleran covering the Rocky Mountains and the Laurentide, centered on Hudson Bay but covering most of eastern Canada. Between these two ice sheets an ice-free corridor opened up through which hunters could have found a way to the Great Plains. When this corridor opened and when people first passed through it are at present uncertain. The earliest evidence of human occupation south of the ice sheets which has stood up to scrutiny (most has not) comes from the Meadowcroft rock shelter in Pennsylvania which has produced evidence of occupation from as early as 16,000 BP. This is older than any evidence of occupation so far discovered in Alaska and it is very difficult to explain where these people could have come from or what became of them. The main migration, that of the Paleo-Indians, did not take place until around 11,500 years ago, after which there is a continuous record of human occupation in the Americas. The arrival of the Paleo-Indians is marked by

Below: The melting of the great transcontinental ice sheets of North America *c.* 11,500 years ago opened a land route along which the Paleo-Indians traveled to reach the game-filled Great Plains.

finds of beautifully worked fluted spear-heads, known as Clovis points after an important archeological site in New Mexico, at sites from Alaska to Mexico. The Clovis points were among the most deadly of any Stone Age weapons and were quite capable of inflicting a fatal wound even on a mammoth, though the Paleo-Indians generally preferred smaller game. The Paleo-Indians spread through the Americas with astonishing speed. By about 11,150 BP Paleo-Indians had entered Mexico and 150 years later they had crossed the Isthmus of Panama into South America: by 10,700 BP they had reached Patagonia, almost at the southern tip of South America.

Early man's progress around the world was marked by a wave of mass extinctions. In Eurasia mammoths, woolly rhino, giant deer, and cave bears became extinct. In Australia giant kangaroos and wombats, marsupial wolves and diprotodon (a rhinoceros-like marsupial) were among many species that became extinct within a few thousand years of the arrival of humans. Shortly after humans arrived in the Americas, dozens of species of mammal, including the mammoth, horse, camel, mastodon (American elephant), ground sloth, and giant armadillo became extinct. In Polynesia dozens of species of flightless birds, including the 9-feet tall giant moa of New Zealand, vanished soon after human settlement. The climatic and habitat changes caused by the end of glacial conditions must have played a part in some of these extinctions but over-hunting was the decisive factor in most areas, especially the Americas where Paleo-Indian hunters are known often to have killed far more animals than they could use. It is no coincidence that Africa has (but for how long?) a more varied fauna of large mammals than any other continent. Humans and wildlife evolved in balance alongside each other in Africa: outside Africa wildlife did not have time to evolve strategies for coping with human predation before many species were hunted to extinction.

Right: Prehistoric Aboriginal petroglyph of an emu, Tasmania. Tasmania was first settled by humans *c.* 30,000 years ago when the island was linked to Australia by a land-bridge: the most southerly place to be occupied by humans before the end of the Ice Age.

Below: Africa possesses the most diverse fauna of large mammals. Humans and wildlife evolved in balance in Africa, but when humans moved out of Africa they encountered animal species which had never experienced human predation: many species were hunted to extinction before they could evolve strategies to cope.

CHAPTER SEVEN

The Revolution of the Upper Paleolithic

About 40,000-50,000 years ago the development of language revolutionized the way humans thought and communicated. Great changes in human behavior become evident in the archeological record: evidence for art and music, symbolic and abstract thought, religion, and new orders of technological innovation become widespread while the human population of the world increased greatly. Archeologists classify the period 40,000-10,000 BP, in which these changes took place, as the Upper Paleolithic, the last phase of the "Old" Stone Age. The region where the results of this revolution in human behavior can be seen at their most spectacular is Europe. This is not because the Upper Paleolithic Europeans took the lead in humanity's cultural development – similar developments occurred quite independently in many other places – but because Europe's prehistory has been far more intensively investigated than any other region's.

One of the characteristics of the Paleolithic revolution is a move toward miniaturization in toolmaking. The arrival of modern humans in Europe is marked by the appearance in the archeological record of a new style of toolmaking based on the production of long thin blades of a standardized size and shape. Though this new technique was

Below: The dangers of the hunt – a wounded bison, its entrails spilling out, attacks one of its hunters, Lascaux, *c.* 15,000 years old.

demanding, it could produce three to 12 times the length of cutting edge from the same weight of stone as the Neanderthals' Mousterian flake-producing technique. The blade was extremely versatile as it could be used as the basis of a very wide range of tools, from knives and projectile points, scrapers for cleaning hides, and borers and burins (engravers) for working antler and bone. Because these tools were small and light, large numbers of them could be carried and used for different tasks as required, rather like the different blades of a Swiss Army knife. Bone needles appear for the first time, showing that the moderns could make much more sophisticated clothing than the Neanderthals.

Tool types give important clues about the nature of the modern humans' settlement of Europe. The earliest style of tools associated with modern humans in Europe, known as the Aurignacian, dates from between 30,000 and 40,000 years ago and is found over a wide area from the Balkans to Spain. However, during the remainder of the Upper Paleolithic many regional and even local

Upper Paleolithic

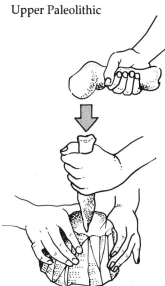

Above: Upper Paleolithic toolmakers could manufacture dozens of parallel-sided blades from a single core using a punch and hammer. These blades could be retouched to make a wide variety of tools.

Left: Flint burins made from retouched blades were used for engraving bone, antler, ivory, and wood. They are one of the most typical tools of the Upper Paleolithic.

styles developed. What this pattern seems to indicate is that the first modern humans to move into Europe came from a single homogenous group. Descendants of this group spread rapidly across Europe taking their distinctive tool kit with them but as they settled down into relatively isolated populations, differences began to develop (cultural evolution paralleling physical evolution in this respect). These differences are stylistic rather than functional, so they probably served as badges of ethnic or tribal identity, expressing each group's awareness of itself as a distinct social unit. Some tools, such as the laurel-leaf blades of the French Solutrean culture (22,000-16,000 BP), were so finely worked that they were probably intended to be display objects or gifts to be exchanged at festivals to cement alliances between groups or individuals.

The period of initial colonization of Europe by modern humans was relatively mild by Ice Age standards. Ice sheets covered all of Scandinavia, most of the British Isles (which were linked to the continent by the low sea levels), the Alps, and the Pyrenees but though

winters were much colder than those of today, summer temperatures were only a little lower. Most of Europe that was not covered with ice was tundra or steppe with sparse woodland in sheltered valleys: forests were confined to the Mediterranean area. Though not as rich in game as tropical savannah, these open grasslands supported large herds of horse, reindeer, bison, woolly rhino, and mammoth. These herds followed regular migration routes through southwestern France, southern Germany, and the Volga basin in Russia and it was in these areas that the newcomers settled most densely. Europe was not uninhabited, Neanderthal man had been living there for tens of thousands of years already, but there was probably little conflict between them and the newcomers as the two groups had different hunting strategies. A very wide range of animal remains is found at Neanderthal sites, showing that they were opportunistic hunters who took whatever was going at the time. The moderns on the other hand were specialists: at their sites it is not unusual for over 90 percent of animal

Above: Blade tools of the Upper Paleolithic Solutrean culture, Saône-et-Loire, France, *c.* 21,000 years old: an end-scraper (*top left*); burins (*center left and below left*); projectile point (*above center*); fine scraper (*below center*); scraper (*top right and center right*); projectile point (*below right*).

Other than berries in season, plant foods were very scarce and if the reindeer or horses unpredictably migrated by a different route one year, the people who depended on them would be in dire trouble. Some degree of protection was gained by developing long-distance exchange systems which traded high-quality flint for toolmaking and luxuries like seashells and amber for making body ornaments. These systems no doubt exchanged information as well as materials and gave early warning of unusual herd movements. Perhaps these contacts helped maintain mutually beneficial agreements to

Below: A finely worked Solutrean projectile point. These exquisite objects were too fragile to have been intended for practical use; they were probably made for display or prestige gift exchanges.

remains to belong to one species only. In western Europe reindeer and horse were the most commonly hunted animals, on the more open steppelands of eastern Europe it was mammoth and reindeer.

One of the most important innovations of the Upper Paleolithic was the spear thrower. This is a simple device (still used by modern hunter-gatherers, such as the Aborigines) for increasing the arc traveled by the arm in the act of throwing a spear, greatly increasing its range and force: used against closely packed herds of migrating animals it was deadly. The carefully targeted strategy of the moderns was much more efficient than the hit-and-miss strategy of the Neanderthals who were few in numbers even before the moderns arrived. In the most favored areas of southwestern France the hunting strategy of the moderns could support a population density that was as much as 10 times higher than that of the Neanderthals. In the face of such effective competition for resources, the Neanderthals simply found themselves squeezed out.

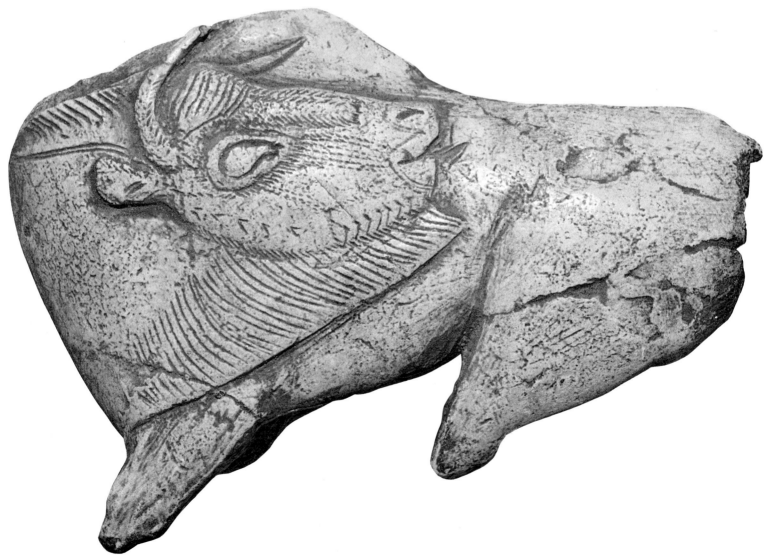

share hunting grounds if migration routes changed, such as are found among some modern tribes of caribou hunters in northern Canada. Some mechanisms for securing marriage partners from other groups will also have been necessary to prevent interbreeding.

The Upper Paleolithic people preferred to live in sheltered valleys close to fords which perhaps were used as regular crossing places by migrating herds. Where possible they chose south-facing caves or rock shelters to catch the warmth of the sun as much as possible. Tents and screens of hide were built to make these draughty sites more comfortable. In areas like central Europe and the steppes of the Ukraine and Russia where there was little shelter and no trees, sturdy huts were built of mammoth bones on promontories overlooking rivers. One of the most important of these sites, at Mezhirich in the Ukraine, was occupied between 18,000 and 14,000 BP, the coldest period of the last glaciation. The settlement consisted of five round huts, varying in size from 13 to 22 feet (4-7m) in diameter. The huts were built with an intricate framework of mammoth bones and were probably covered with mammoth hide. Building the huts required a major investment of labor and would have taken 10 men five or six days to complete. Such substantial and skillfully constructed structures surely deserve to be regarded as architecture. Between the huts, pits dug into the permafrost were used as deep freezers for storing meat. Despite the harsh climate, these steppe dwellers flourished: Mezhirich had a population of about 50 while another Ukrainian site, a tented village at Kostenki, may have had a population of hundreds. Many Upper Paleolithic sites in France, such as at La Madeleine, also accommodated groups that were far larger than any found from earlier periods. Clearly, Upper Paleolithic societies were far more complex than earlier human societies but there are few clues as to their exact nature, though modern hunter-gatherer societies, (see next chapter) may give some clues.

Though a few Neanderthal burials are known, it is only in the Upper Paleolithic that human burials become common. Many

Top left: Upper Paleolithic engraving from Gabillou, France, of a woman wearing an anorak. Unlike the Neanderthals, modern humans were not adapted to cold climates but could survive because of their ability to make warm clothing.

Below left: This bone carving of a bison licking its flank shows an intimate knowledge of the animal's behavior. La Madeleine, France, *c.* 14,000 years old.

Below: The Dordogne river, southwestern France, was a favored area of settlement for Upper Paleolithic man because of its many caves and rock shelters and because it lay across major animal migration routes.

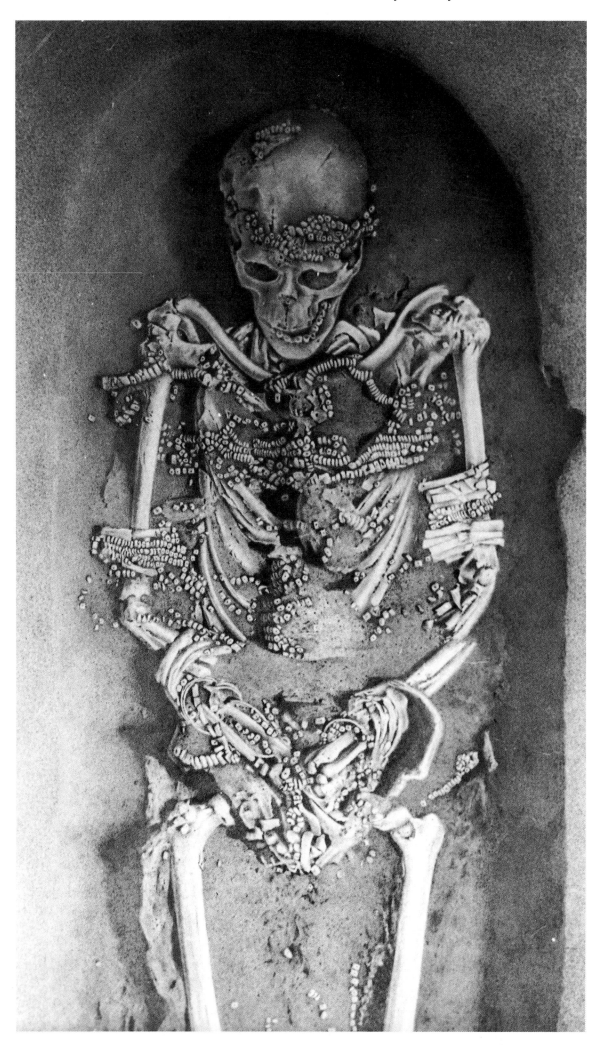

Left: Male burial, Sungir near Moscow, *c.* 24,000 years old. The man was apparently buried in a hooded jacket which was richly decorated with beads of mammoth ivory. The presence of personal ornaments and tools in Upper Paleolithic burials is probably indicative of a belief in an afterlife.

of these burials include grave goods, which presumably indicates a belief in some kind of afterlife. Skeletons from three burials at Sungir, north of Moscow, were covered with thousands of ivory beads which appeared to have been sewn on to a hooded garment rather like a parka. Two of the burials included stone tools and ivory carvings. Another skeleton from a burial at Arene Candide in northern Italy was decorated with seashells and tools made from antlers. Skeletons from Cro-Magnon and La Madeleine in France have been found decorated with shell necklaces and bracelets, others have been found with bears' teeth pendants. This concern with personal decoration is itself something new to the Upper Paleolithic and is a sign of man's new self-awareness. We also know from carvings from Brassempouy and Willendorf that Upper Paleolithic women had elaborate hairstyles.

The Upper Paleolithic of Europe is best known for its remarkable artistic achievements. Upper Paleolithic art falls into two distinct types: portable art and cave art. Portable art is the most widespread, being found from the Ukraine to Spain but cave art is virtually confined to northern Spain and southwestern France. The absence of cave art from some areas, like the Ukraine, is no mystery – there are no caves – but its absence from other areas of central Europe where caves are common is harder to explain.

The first art appears around 32,000 years ago, a few thousand years earlier than any

Left: The so-called Venus of Willendorf, Austria *c.* 25,000 years old. Clay or ivory figurines of naked women with exaggerated breasts and buttocks have been found across Europe from the Pyrenees to the Ukraine. Their meaning and purpose is unknown but they may be related to a widespread fertility cult. This Venus has an elaborate hairstyle but, typically, no details of her face have been carved.

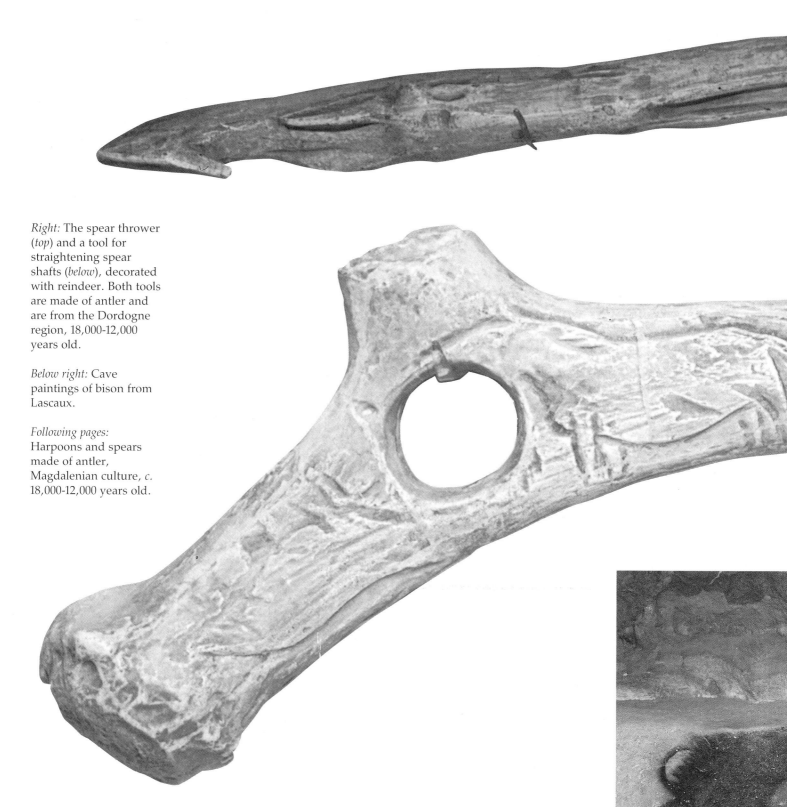

Right: The spear thrower (*top*) and a tool for straightening spear shafts (*below*), decorated with reindeer. Both tools are made of antler and are from the Dordogne region, 18,000-12,000 years old.

Below right: Cave paintings of bison from Lascaux.

Following pages: Harpoons and spears made of antler, Magdalenian culture, *c.* 18,000-12,000 years old.

surviving art found elsewhere in the world. At first artists made only simple paintings and engravings of animals and human sexual organs, but by 25,000 BP they were blowing or brushing pigment around their hands to make imprints on cave walls. Around this time too the remarkable so-called "Stone-Age Venus" figurines were fashioned. These are sculpted figurines and bas-reliefs of females with greatly exaggerated breasts and buttocks and usually without hands, feet, and faces. Some appear to be pregnant. Whatever their actual sig-

nificance (they are usually explained as fertility symbols), the Venus figurines were associated with a widespread set of beliefs as they are found across Europe from the Ukraine to France.

The greatest period of Upper Paleolithic art, the Magdalenian (named after the important site at La Madeleine), began about 18,000 years ago at the height of the last glaciation. This is the period of the stunning cave murals from Lascaux in France, Altamira in Spain, and other sites, but a wealth of portable art, from ivory carvings to

decorated spear throwers, was also created. Cave art is almost entirely devoted to depictions of animals. The style is vigorous, naturalistic, and shows great attention to detail, making it easy to identify the subjects. The repertoire is extensive: for example, the 14,000-year-old cave paintings at Altamira show bison, aurochs, deer, ibex, chamois, mammoth, cat, and wild boar as well as abstract symbols. The range of colors was limited to reds, browns, yellows, and blacks as the main pigments used were limited to red-brown iron ocher and black manganese dioxide. Techniques were simple: paint was made by mixing the pigments in water and was applied to the cave wall by being sprayed from the artist's mouth. The artists had no understanding of perspective and subjects are shown in profile (portable art shows a greater range of postures). Human figures are very rare but include pictures of men dressed in animal skins wearing horns or antlers on their heads. These are thought to represent shamans or witch doctors. Cave art came to an end 11,000 years ago when the Ice Age began to end and force a new way of life on the Magdalenians.

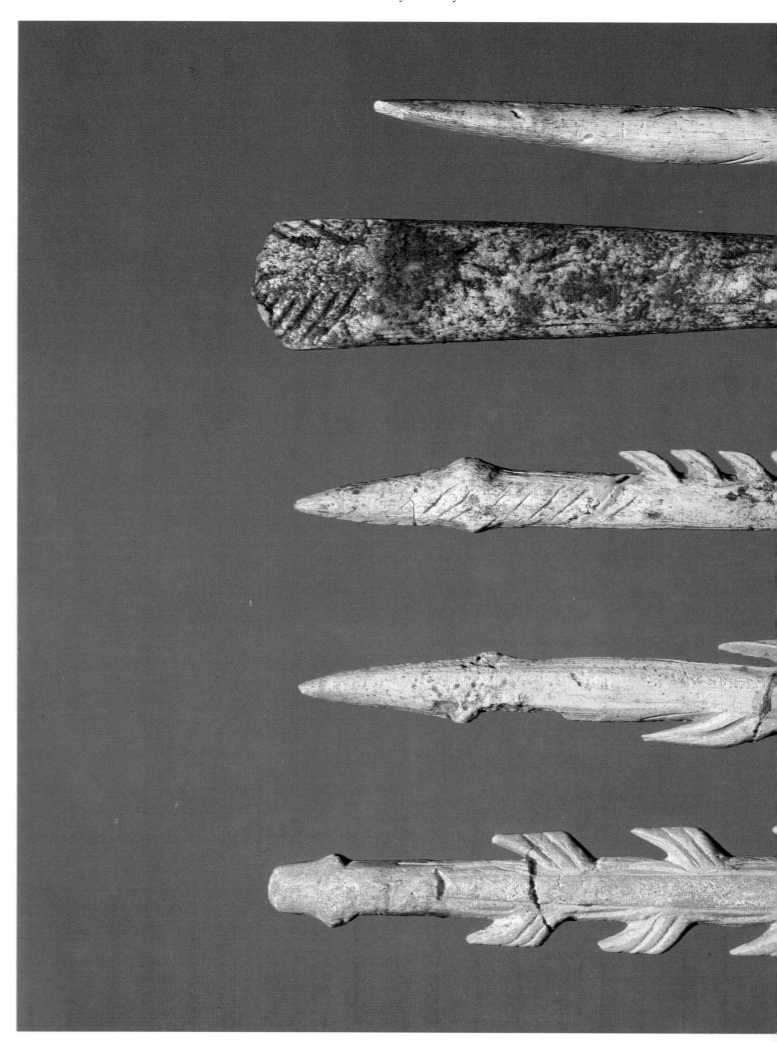

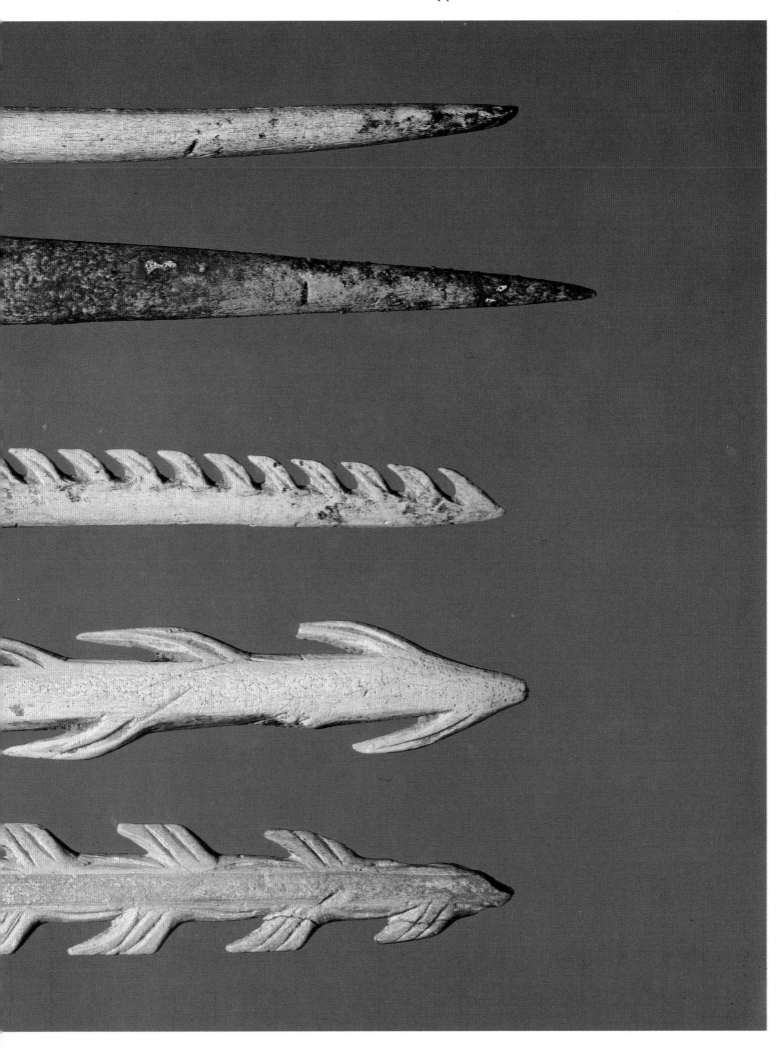

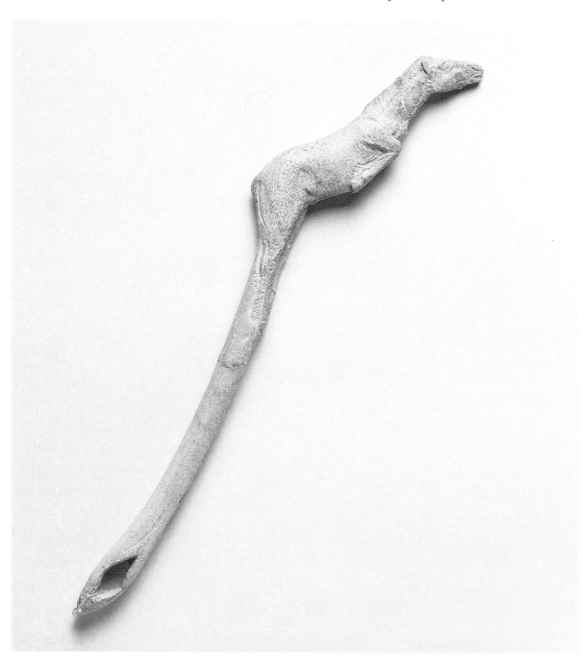

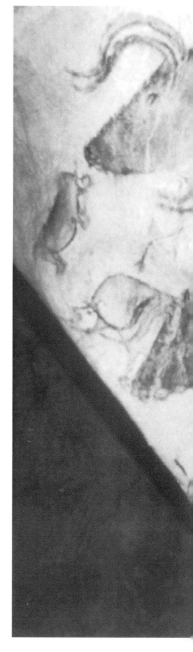

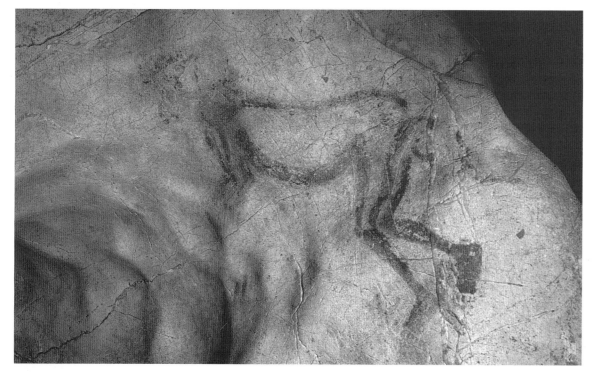

Above left: Magdalenian spear thrower decorated with a leaping horse, Bruniquel, southwestern France.

Left: Human figures rarely appear in cave art, those that do, often seem to have a ritual or religious meaning such as this figure, interpreted as a shaman, from the Grotte des Trois Frères in southern France.

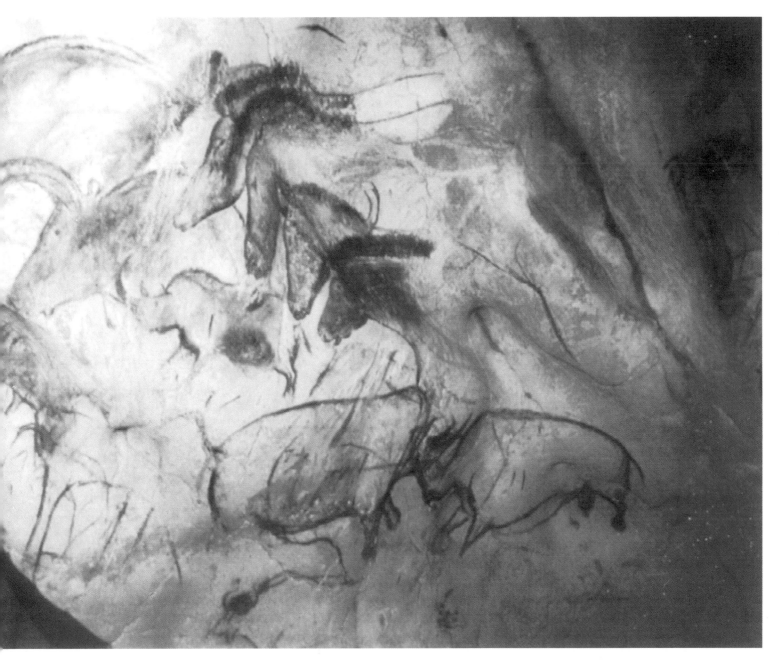

The meaning of the cave paintings has been endlessly discussed but at the end of the day all interpretations are necessarily speculative. Paintings are often superimposed on one another without regard for the work of earlier artists or for compositional effect. This suggests that the end result was not as important as the actual act of depiction, thus it was not art for art's sake. Most of the animals depicted are known to have been preyed on by the Magdalenians so the cave paintings could be some kind of sympathetic magic intended to multiply the herds or otherwise aid hunting. Probably the most widely accepted explanation is that the paintings represent totemic animals associated with shamanistic rituals. The positions of the paintings are also seen as being potentially significant. Some chambers seem to have been chosen for painting because of unusual acoustic prop-

erties. Other paintings are in very inaccessible places up to 1000 yards (914m) underground so perhaps the difficulty of reaching them somehow added to their significance, perhaps as part of an initiation ritual. Some abstract patterns have been interpreted as records of environmental and calendrical information such as the phases of the moon. Whatever their actual meaning, the real significance of the cave paintings is that they show that Upper Paleolithic man had a fully modern capacity for symbolic thought. The people of the Upper Paleolithic knew far less about the world than we do but they were just as intelligent as us and just as capable. An Upper Paleolithic child could, if miraculously transported to our own time, be taught to read and write, operate a computer, drive a car, or perform any of the other complex activities which form part of our daily lives.

Above: Spectacular cave paintings showing horses, buffalo, and rhinoceroses discovered in 1994 near Vallon-Pont-d'Arc, Ardèche, southern France, *c.* 20,000 years old.

CHAPTER EIGHT

A Window on the Past: Modern Hunter-Gatherers

Paleolithic humans all depended on hunting and gathering to provide the essentials of life. Many of these Paleolithic hunter-gatherer groups have left rich archeological remains, but there is only so much that these can tell us about an ancient pre-literate society. Interpreting artifacts which had a symbolic meaning, such as art, a burial, or a ritual structure, is very difficult because the people whose minds carried and understood that meaning are gone. At least with artifacts we can see what they looked like and make an intelligent guess at their meaning or purpose but some of the most important aspects of human behavior leave few material traces. How were Paleolithic hunting parties organized? What kind of family structures did they have? How did they see their place in the world? What were relations between the sexes like? How were disputes settled? The list could be a long one.

One way to get an insight into the ways of life of Paleolithic hunters and gatherers is by drawing analogies from the behavior of the few hunter-gatherer societies which survived into the modern age. Anthropologists recognize two types of hunter-gatherer societies, the nomadic "generalized hunter-gatherer" and the rarer sedentary "complex hunter-gatherer." All Paleolithic hunter-gatherers were of the generalized variety, complex hunter-gatherer societies did not evolve until after the Ice Age (see chapter 9).

We need to be careful in the conclusions we draw from modern hunter-gatherer societies. Although the generalized hunter-gatherer way of life is well over a million years old, it is not static. The behavior of hunter-gatherers is in fact very flexible and adaptive (it has to be) and their customs, habits, and beliefs may often be of relatively recent origin. Modern generalized hunter-

Modern hunter-gatherer art, like Upper Paleolithic art, is often concerned with the all-important activity of hunting: Eskimo hunting caribou with bows and arrows (*below*), Eskimo hunting a whale in an umiak (*below right*) – engravings on walrus ivory, nineteenth century AD, and (*above right*) San Bushman cave paintings of antelope, Matopos, Zimbabwe, date uncertain.

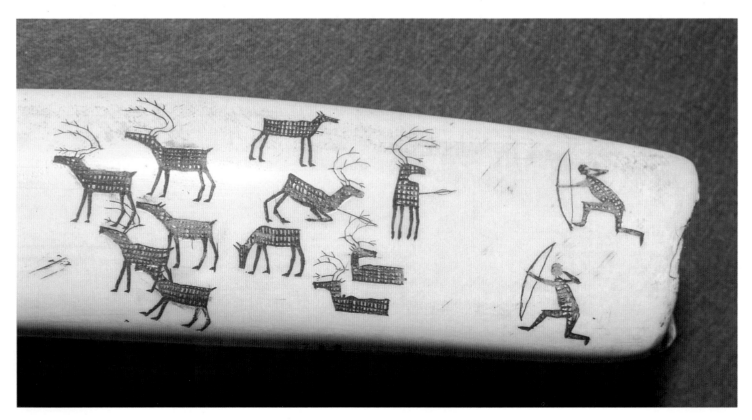

gatherers are largely confined to environments which Paleolithic man would have regarded as marginal, such as rainforests, coniferous forests, and deserts. Arctic hunters, like the Inuit, live in conditions which are not dissimilar to those which must have been experienced by Upper Paleolithic man in Europe and Siberia but most of the big game which flourished on the Ice Age tundras is now extinct. Modern hunter-gatherers may then live more uncertain lives than the majority of their Paleolithic forebears did. However, modern generalized hunter-gatherers do share the same basic problems that faced Paleolithic hunter-gatherers, so it is likely that they also shared similar social and economical arrangements. "Shared" is the operative word because there are now no pristine hunter-gatherer societies left in the world: those few peoples who continue to live in this way have all in recent decades been exposed to the strong and usually destructive and demoralizing influence of Western civilization.

For many centuries, hunter-gatherers were believed by Europeans to lead lives of extreme hardship and deprivation. According to the seventeenth-century English philosopher Thomas Hobbes their state could be summarized thus: "No arts; no letters; no society; and which is worse of all, continual fear and danger of a violent death; and the life of man, solitary, poor, nasty, brutish, and short." Therefore, when anthropologists finally began to take hunter-gatherer societies seriously in the post-war period, it came as something of a shock to discover that their lives were not like that at all. Hunter-gatherers rarely went short of food and what was more, even in the marginal environments to which they had been confined by the twentieth century, they did not have to work very hard to get it. The Dobe !Kung people of the Kalahari desert, for instance, are able to provide all the basics of life for themselves by about two to three hours work a day, depending on the season. The rest of their time is to be spent at leisure, either gossiping and socializing, telling stories, playing games, or resting. This compares very favorably with the modern affluent lifestyle in which commuting, shopping, cooking, and household chores must be added to a 40-hour working week before leisure can begin. Not for nothing, though with some exaggeration, have the hunter-gatherers been styled the "first affluent society."

Above: Modern San Bushmen under the painted overhang of a rock shelter in the Kalahari desert. Paintings survive well in the dry desert climate and range in date from 15,000 BC to the nineteenth century AD. San art, much of which is concerned with shamanistic ritual, has had a considerable influence on our understanding of Paleolithic cave art.

Right: Dobe !Kung Bushman equipped for a hunting trip with a bow and quiver of arrows.

Above: Hunter-gatherers in tropical climates travel light. The human figures in this Aboriginal painting from Kakadu, Northern Territories, are carrying dilly bags which contain their few possessions.

Left: Australian Aborigine, Northern Territories, cooking a kangaroo. In most hunter-gatherer societies the hunter does not have exclusive rights over his kill, it must be shared between the whole band.

Hunter-gatherer affluence has been achieved by social adaptations which are designed to suppress competition for resources. Competition, so we are told, is a good thing in an industrialized society but it is potentially deadly to the hunter-gatherer. The main problem faced by hunter-gatherers is how to obtain reliable food supplies in a world where the availability of plants and animals is unpredictably variable. Hunter-gatherers are totally dependent on the natural productivity of the environment, they cannot, as farming or industrialized peoples can, step up production to meet increased demand. Uncontrolled demand for resources would quickly lead to their over-exploitation and starvation for all (this may yet happen to our industrialized society, of course). Hunter-gatherers therefore limit population growth and have an economic system based on sharing resources to reduce damaging competition.

Hunter-gatherers have learned that if their lifestyle is to be sustainable, they must maintain their numbers well below (usually between 20 and 60 percent of) the theoretical maximum carrying capacity of their environment. This ensures that under normal conditions everyone in the group can live well for very little expenditure of effort and that in bad years nobody starves. In practice this means that hunter-gatherer societies go to great lengths to limit their population by discouraging early marriage, weaning infants late to suppress fertility, and exposing surplus babies. The latter might seem harsh but parents know that the survival of their existing children could be threatened by too many new mouths to feed. Also, generalized hunter-gatherer bands need to be mobile and it is impractical for a mother to have more than one infant to carry at a time. These measures are usually successful in restraining population growth below 0.001 percent per year and typically hunter-gatherer population densities are very low. A tundra environment, for instance, can sustain a theoretical maximum hunter-gatherer density of no more than 0.05 people per km^2 (0.3861 square miles) and in practice only 20-60 percent of this. Put another way, a band of 30 Inuit caribou hunters would need a range of around 3000km^2 (1158.3 square miles). Even in richer environments such as savannahs, steppes, prairies, and the game-rich tundras of Upper Paleolithic Europe, population densities could rarely have exceeded 0.1 people per km^2 (i.e. a band would still need

Left: Australian Aborigine using a spear thrower. The design of this simple but highly effective device has not changed since Upper Paleolithic times – see the illustration on page 74.

Below: Aborigine using a boomerang, an aerodynamically shaped throwing stick. Though the Aboriginal boomerang is unique in that it returns to the thrower if it fails to find a target, similar throwing sticks were widely used by other hunter-gatherers in India, North America, and North Africa.

around 300km^2). Historically, their small numbers and need for a great deal of space has made hunter-gatherers very vulnerable to encroachment by more numerous farming peoples, to the extent that the hunter-gatherer way of life is now almost extinct.

The typical unit of social organization among generalized hunter-gatherers is the band. Bands are usually between 30 and 50 strong. A larger band than this would exhaust the local food sources so quickly that it would be forever on the move; a smaller band would find it hard to raise enough adult men for a successful hunting party. Archeological sites from many parts of the world show that this has been the average band size since at least Upper Paleolithic times. Bands are always egalitarian and exhibitionist behavior or attempts to coerce other band members against their will are always suppressed. Because of their power to communicate with the spirit world, shamans or witch-doctors are normally the most feared and influential people in hunter-gatherer society. All food and property is shared within the band and if anyone asks for anything, it is always willingly given. This is not generosity but enlightened self-interest. A hunter will, on

average, make a kill only once every 4-10 days. If a hunter kept the whole of his kill to himself, he would have more than he could eat some of the time and nothing at all at others. By sharing his kill with others, the hunter can be confident that others will do the same with him: if he has a run of bad luck he knows that he will not go hungry nor is he forced to compete for game with other band members, so reducing the chances of over-hunting. Some people inevitably contribute more food than others but anyone who abuses the system and tries to live off the labor of others will simply be excluded from the band.

Generalized hunter-gatherers do not belong to tribes as such (by definition a tribe has leadership) but bands do form wide-ranging alliances with other bands. These alliances serve the same function at an inter-band level as food-sharing does within the band: it suppresses competition for resources and evens out irregularities in food supplies. If one band has a bumper crop of nuts or other plant food in its territory, it will invite allied bands to come and share it. Likewise, if animal migration routes change unexpectedly, a band will share its hunting

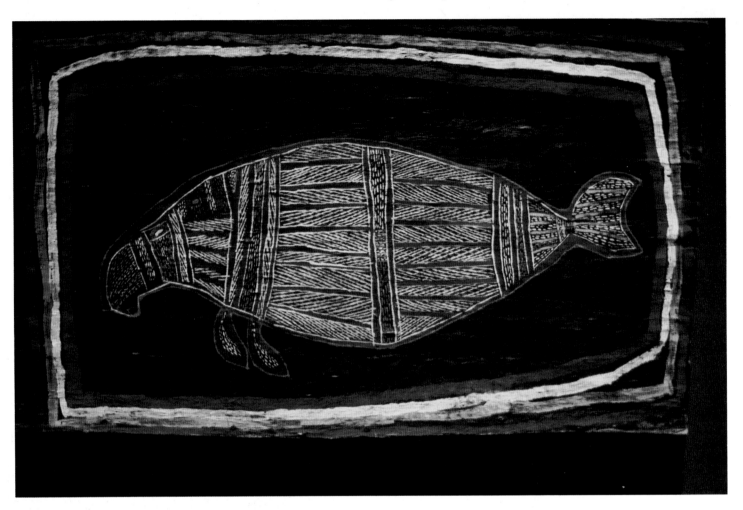

grounds with its allies, as the Chippewayan Indians of Canada did. If a band is faced with a critical food shortage in its own territory, it can simply go and visit an allied band and ask to be fed. These alliances are essential to the survival of hunter-gatherer bands in bad years and they are continually maintained by a complex social life. All the bands may come together for a short time every year to celebrate religious festivals. Shamanistic rituals induce an ecstatic trance-like condition in worshippers and shared religious experiences of this kind create particularly strong emotional ties between individuals. Festivals were also occasions to exchange gifts of stone for toolmaking and luxuries like decorative seashells or beads. It is thought that some of the most important sites of Upper Paleolithic cave art in Europe served as similar ritual centers. There is also a constant to-ing and fro-ing of visitors between bands during the year, maintaining individual friendships. European settlers in Australia misinterpreted the Aboriginal habit of "going walkabout" as mere aimless wandering, when it was in fact an important part of their adaptive strategy. Another means of cementing alliances is by arranging marriages to create kinship links between bands. So important is this that it is rare for hunter-

gatherer societies to permit marriage within the band (this helps prevent inbreeding too).

Disputes over women are the most common cause when alliances break down. Violence is usually limited and peace is easily patched up as soon as one side has proved itself the stronger. Feuds with bands outside the alliance network are not uncommon and though they are rarely prosecuted with great vigor, hostilities can continue for generations. Disputes within bands are usually settled by peer group pressure but in serious cases the dissident minority may leave to join another band or try to survive alone. Crime is virtually unknown and there is no motive for theft as one only has to ask for something for it to be given and it is, in any case, impossible to accumulate more possessions than can be carried. Violently disruptive people may be expelled from the group, in which case they would probably starve, or in extreme cases they might be killed by their fellows.

The technology of hunter-gatherers is determined largely by the environment and the need for mobility. Most hunter-gatherers need to move on to find new food sources about once a month, so they cannot acquire much in the way of possessions and their technology must be lightweight and

Above: Aboriginal bark painting of a dugong. Bark paintings feature totemic animals and designs and were used in rituals to maintain contact between humans and mythic spirits which created the world. If the rituals ceased to be performed, the Aborigines believed that the wildlife would leave the land.

Right: Cree Indian woman near Hudson Bay, Canada, cleaning caribou hide with a bone scraper mounted in a heavy wooden handle. Upper Paleolithic end-scrapers may have been used in a similar way. Hunter-gatherer societies have well-defined roles for men and women: cleaning hides is women's work.

easily portable. This is not a problem for those living in warm climates as they need neither clothes nor shelter: an Aborigine needs only spears, spear thrower, throwing sticks, and bags to carry a few tools. On the other hand, to cope with the demanding arctic environment, the Inuit's survival depends on a complex technology of spears, bows, harpoons, fishing tackle, multi-layered clothing, stone cooking pots, sledges, and skin boats. However, as they can store food easily they do not need to be as mobile as other hunter-gatherers. It is not surprising that in warm climates hunter-gatherers waste little effort building shelters which they know they will soon abandon but this is also the case in cold climates. For example the Athabascan Indians of the Yukon relied only on surprisingly flimsy tents to survive savage winter weather. Only relatively sedentary hunter-gatherers, like the Northwest Coast Indians of North America who exploit rich salmon rivers, build substantial dwellings. The same is true of artistic traditions. Many hunter-gatherers from Upper Paleolithic Europe to twentieth-century Australia have painted cave walls, and body ornaments are almost universal, but only complex sedentary hunter-gatherer societies have developed any monumental art. For a long time, the simplicity of hunter-gatherer technology blinded Europeans to the richness of these peoples' oral traditions of myth and storytelling, which are often very sophisticated.

Generalized hunter-gatherers exploit the widest possible range of food sources as insurance against any one of them failing. The Dobe !Kung could recognize over a hundred plant foods and could order them in a hierarchy from most to least nutritious. As far as possible, the most nutritious foods, such as the mongomongo nut (enough of which can be gathered and processed in half an hour or so to provide a day's nutrition), were exploited first and the least nutritious only in times of hardship. Maintaining a correct balance of protein and carbohydrate in the diet is essential because proteins cannot be digested properly without the energy provided from carbohydrates: it would be quite possible to starve to death on a diet which consisted only of lean meat. Obtaining carbohydrates is relatively easy for hunter-gatherers in tropical environments where a wide range of seeds, nuts, and roots is available, but it is a greater problem in higher latitudes where most carbohydrates must come from animal fat. By late winter wild animals

are carrying very little fat, so hunters suffer annual carbohydrate crises until animals begin to fatten again on spring growth. The Upper Paleolithic hunters of Europe must certainly have experienced similar problems. As wild animals always carry less fat than domestic animals, even at the best of times fat may be in short supply and it is always eaten with relish by hunter-gatherers. The hunters with the least problems on this score are the Inuit on the shores of the Arctic Ocean who obtain enough fat from the blubber of marine mammals not only to eat but to provide winter heat and light.

In tropical environments where food is available all year round, hunter-gatherers rarely store food even overnight, such is their confidence in their knowledge of the environment. In higher latitudes storage becomes essential and hunter-gatherers had to learn to dry meat and fish for winter supplies. Arctic dwellers like the Inuit are the most fortunate hunter-gatherers in this respect as almost unlimited amounts of food can be stored in natural deep freezes such as pits dug in the permafrost.

Men and women in hunter-gatherer societies have clearly differentiated roles: the men hunt while the women, whose child rearing responsibilities make them less mobile, gather vegetable foods near the camp. In tropical environments where plant foods are abundant, it is the women who provide most of the band's food. Among the Dobe !Kung the men spend more time talking about hunting than actually doing it but the women gather every day. Nevertheless, despite the fundamental importance of plant foods to the !Kung, meat is regarded as the most prestigious food by both men and women. Away from the tropics where plant foods are very seasonal, or even absent altogether, it is the men who provide most of the food. The (now extinct) Yahgan people of Tierra del Fuego had few plant foods but in coastal areas the women were able to make a significant contribution of food by gathering shellfish on the seashore. Among the Inuit, who have no plant foods at all, virtually 100 percent of the food is provided by the men (the women have plenty of other work to occupy their time, however). This division of labor is likely to be of very long standing and was probably a characteristic of early hominid societies. Apart from the different sex roles, there are no other specialized roles in generalized hunter-gatherer societies, everybody, even the shamans, must be a jack-of-all-trades.

Right and below: Life in a Cree Indian tent. Even in the harsh environment of northern Canada, hunter-gatherers enjoy considerable leisure time to spend socializing or relaxing (*right*). Hunter-gatherers in high latitudes have few plant foods so, unlike those in warmer climates, their diet is made up almost entirely of meat (*below*).

CHAPTER NINE
The World After the Ice

Global warming is very much a current concern. Average temperatures are predicted to increase by one or two degrees celsius over the next century: if they do, weather patterns will change, mountain glaciers and polar ice sheets will retreat, and sea levels may rise by several feet with serious consequences for coastal communities. However, the warming which we may now be experiencing is slight compared to that experienced by our ancestors at the end of the Ice Age 10,000 years ago. The last glaciation reached its peak of cold 18,000 years ago and began a slow amelioration about 14,000 BP. Around 13,000 BP the climate began to warm up more quickly only to relapse back into glacial conditions a thousand years later. This cold snap came to a sudden end 10,000 years ago as temperatures began to rise at a rate of as much as one degree celsius per decade in some parts of the northern hemisphere: within the space of only 700 years most of the terrestrial ice sheets had vanished.

Global warming continued more slowly for about 2000 years after the ice sheets had gone into permanent retreat, until average temperatures were slightly above those of the present day. This period of warmer climate, known as the "climatic optimum" lasted until about 6000 BP, when a slow deterioration set in which brought average temperatures closer to those of the present day by about 5000 BP. The final retreat of the ice sheets marks the end of the Pleistocene geological epoch and the beginning of the Holocene or Present epoch. It also marks the end of the Paleolithic period of human prehistory. The subsequent period is known as the Mesolithic (Middle Stone Age) in Eurasia and the Archaic in the Americas. In most parts of the world, the Mesolithic (or its local equivalent) was a period of transition between the big-game hunting way of life of the Paleolithic and the adoption of farming.

As the ice sheets melted after 10,000 BP they returned their water to the oceans causing sea levels to rise rapidly, submerging huge areas of productive lowland plains. Rainfall increased and forests spread. These rapid changes were a serious problem for the human race. Man's preferred environments, the tropical savannahs, temperate steppes and prairies, and subarctic tundras, all shrank before the advancing forests and rising sea levels. Those groups that could, moved into areas that had previously been uninhabitable because of excessive aridity or ice cover. Increased rainfall meant that most of the Sahara desert gave way to hospitable savannah, while in Europe and North America hunter-gatherers followed the herds north in the wake of the retreating ice sheets in an effort to preserve their traditional way of life. Scandinavia and the British Isles both received their first anatomically modern human inhabitants in this way. Areas which had been densely settled during the Upper Paleolithic, such as southwestern France and northern Spain, now became depopulated. On the Great Plains of

Below: Reconstruction of the Mesolithic camp at Mount Sandel, Northern Ireland, at the Ulster History Park. In the Mesolithic period, hunter-gatherers in many parts of northern Europe became more sedentary and so took more time and trouble building homes for themselves.

The end of the Ice Age spelled the end of the big-game hunting cultures of the Upper Paleolithic and hunter-gatherers all over the world had to adapt to the changing conditions. In northern Europe this meant adapting to life in dense woodlands where game animals, such as red deer (*top right*) and wild boar (*center*), were smaller and more elusive. The warmer conditions brought a greater range of plant foods such as nuts, berries (*bottom*), and fungi (*top left*) which could be exploited.

Left: The Mesolithic saw the introduction of miniaturized toolkits based on small stone flakes and blades called microliths. These microlithic projectile points from the important Mesolithic site at Star Carr, Yorkshire, England, are only just over an inch long.

Below: Antler harpoon points of the French Azilian culture which developed at the end of the Ice Age. The harpoon points were loosely tied to the shaft.

North America, the extinction of the Ice Age megafauna also led to a population decline and the end of the Clovis big-game hunting culture. However, the survival of the bison enabled many Paleo-Indian groups to continue a big-game hunting lifestyle right up to the nineteenth century AD. Big-game hunting also survived on the northern tundras of America and Eurasia and on the African savannah but in most other parts of the world people had eventually to adapt to the new environmental conditions.

It was not that there was a shortage of food in the post-glacial world, the problem was that it came in smaller packages. The temperate forests of western Europe and the Pacific coast of North America, for example, had rich resources of deer and small mammals, water fowl and seabirds, salmon and marine fish, shellfish, nuts, roots, and berries. The Near East, Far East, and Mesoamerica had plentiful supplies of carbohydrate-rich wild cereals. However, using Upper Paleolithic technology these resources were all time-consuming to exploit. A rabbit is not much easier to catch than a reindeer or bison but

while a reindeer will feed the whole of the hunter-gatherer band for two or three days, a rabbit will not feed one adult for a single day. Wild cereals are time-consuming to harvest and require extensive processing before they can be eaten. Shellfish, though available in vast quantities, have much less nutritional value than meat. Cliff-nesting seabirds can provide eggs and nutritious oily meat but catching them is a dangerous business and needs a good head for heights. Life must have become much more arduous for many hunter-gatherers as the climate became warmer. But, as the saying goes, necessity is the mother of invention and the Mesolithic saw the appearance of a wide range of technological innovations designed to make intensive exploitation of these new food sources easier.

The tendency, begun in the Upper Paleolithic, for miniaturization of tools was continued and many Mesolithic tools were made of tiny blades known as microliths, allowing efficient use of toolmaking stone. Nets, harpoons, pronged fishing spears, fish traps, and boats made fishing an economical proposition for the first time. Nets could also be used for trapping seabirds and water-fowl. Specially shaped tools were used for prising shellfish off rocks. The bow and arrow came into widespread use, allowing fast and accurate shooting at elusive forest animals and birds, while snares and traps took most of the hard work out of catching small game like rabbits. In the Near East rows of sharp microliths were set in handles of wood or bone to make sickles for harvesting wild grains. Grindstones were introduced for processing seeds and nuts.

One of the problems of big-game hunting as a way of life is that large mammals have a slow rate of reproduction and if they have a poor breeding year their numbers can drop catastrophically and take years to recover. For the same reasons they are very vulnerable to over-hunting. For example the Indian hunters of the Great Basin, USA, organized a gazelle drive only once every 10 years because they knew that it took the population that long to recover from the last one. More frequent drives would lead to the local extinction of the gazelle. By contrast, fish,

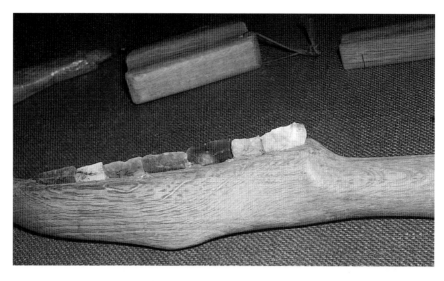

birds, small mammals like rabbits, shellfish, and wild grains all have rapid reproduction rates and breed in huge numbers. What the new technology of the Mesolithic did was allow people to tap into these apparently limitless supplies of food. The human population began to rise and in certain favored areas food resources were so rich that hunter-gatherers needed to move only once a season or could even become completely

Above: Several microliths could be used together to make composite tools such as this reconstruction of a wooden handled saw-knife.

settled. Once hunter-gatherers settled down and it became possible for people to accumulate possessions, it became worthwhile to spend time and effort building permanent dwellings; food surpluses could be stored and, as food was so abundant, sharing was no longer necessary outside the family. A new technology of food storage developed such as racks for drying meat and fish, baskets, and, now that they did not have to be carried around, pots and bowls could be made out of stone. Some sedentary hunter-gatherers, such as the Jomon people of Japan 10,000 year ago, even learned how to make fired clay pots.

Under these circumstances, the absolutely egalitarian structures of generalized hunter-gatherer societies broke down. Because it was now harder to exhaust the local food supplies, people could live together in large groups or tribes. Individuals could now compete with one another to acquire prestige objects and to accumulate stores of surplus food. These food surpluses could be given away at feasts (such as the potlatches held until recently by the Indians of the Northwest Coast of North America) and other occasions,

not out of generosity, but to put the recipients under obligation to the giver. Those who could not reciprocate fully found themselves obliged to pay their debt in other ways, such as by performing services for the giver. In some cases, those who could not reciprocate at all fell completely under the power of the giver and became effectively enslaved to him. In this way, a rudimentary class structure emerged in these sedentary or, as they are known to anthropologists, "complex" hunter-gatherer communities. A certain amount of occupational specialization could also occur: for example, there were specialist boat-builders among the Northwest Coast Indians of America. Another consequence of sedentism was increased territoriality and it is from the Mesolithic that the first evidence of large-scale violence appears. In one Mesolithic cemetery at Sahaba, Sudan, 40 percent of the bodies showed evidence of violent death. Spanish cave paintings show battle scenes, and weapons designed for fighting rather than hunting appear in many areas of the world.

One of the best-documented Mesolithic cultures is that of southern Scandinavia. The

Right: Sedentary hunter-gatherers could begin to accumulate possessions and prestige objects such as this Alaskan Tlingit Indian chief's blanket.

Below: Salish Indian woman smoke-drying salmon, British Columbia. By discovering methods of preserving and storing seasonally abundant food sources, hunter-gatherers could adopt a more sedentary lifestyle.

Following pages: In exceptionally rich environments, hunter-gatherers were able to live in large permanent villages like this late nineteenth-century Kwakiutl Indian village in British Columbia. In the summer, groups dispersed from the village to temporary camps to exploit seasonal food sources.

Mesolithic here lasted from around 10,000 BP, when reindeer hunters moved into the region from the south, to around 5500 BP when the inhabitants adopted farming as a way of life. As the climate grew warmer and the reindeer herds moved still further north, these hunters began to adapt to the new conditions. At first they hunted elk (the European equivalent of moose) and aurochs, both of which supply up to 1000 pounds of meat, but within a few millennia the forests had become too dense for these animals and they disappeared from many areas. The largest animals now available were the red and roe deer and wild boar, and these not in great numbers. The inhabitants were forced to exploit more and more diverse resources to secure a reliable food supply, including much greater use of plant foods.

At the beginning of the period, hunter-gatherers migrated from site to site on a seasonal basis but they became increasingly sedentary as time went on and by around 8000 BP settlements were occupied all year round. Permanent settlements were located in places that bordered on different types of environment such as estuaries, riversides, and lakeshores so that there would be a wide variety of different food resources close by.

Settlements were widely scattered and separated by uninhabited forests and open coasts. Associated with the permanent settlements were smaller temporary camps which were occupied for only a few weeks a year by task groups engaged in specific activities such as fishing, sealing, or wildfowling. Dug-out canoes, sophisticated fish traps, spears, and lightweight arrows for

Far left: Haida Indian totem pole, Queen Charlotte Islands, British Columbia. Freed from the need to move camp every few weeks, sedentary hunter-gatherers could develop rich traditions of non-portable art.

Above: A hunter with a bow pursues a wounded deer in this Mesolithic cave painting from San Joseph, Spain. The bow was better suited to fast and accurate shooting at elusive forest game than the spear and its use became widespread in the Mesolithic.

Left: Triangular and trapezoidal microliths of the French late Mesolithic Tardenoisian culture. These microliths would have served as barbs and tips on arrows.

wildfowling were developed to exploit these resources more efficiently. Around 7000 BP pottery storage jars and cooking pots came into use, probably as a result of contacts with farming peoples in Germany. Heavy wood-working tools like axes and adzes for build-ing houses and boats were also developed.

Evidence that Mesolithic societies in southern Scandinavia had a simple class structure comes from burial practice. Most burials were furnished with artifacts such as tools and body ornaments, but there are wide variations in the number and quality of offerings, suggesting that some people were wealthier or had higher status than others. Polished stone artifacts, like war clubs, which were extremely costly to produce in terms of labor, also appear. These were probably manufactured as prestige objects for high status individuals.

The people of southern Scandinavia were in many ways typical of those in other temperate forest areas: complex hunter-gatherers with very similar social structures and ways of life existed in the British Isles and northeastern North America at around the same time, for example.

Another type of complex hunter-gatherer society, known as the Natufian, developed in the uplands of the Levant around 12,000 BP. As the climate warmed up toward the end of the Ice Age, this region was colonized by plants like wild emmer wheat and wild

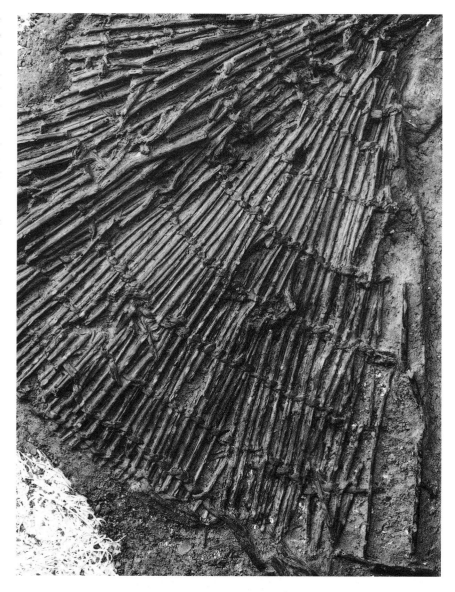

Above: Mesolithic wicker fish trap from Villingbaeke, Denmark. Such traps were designed so that fish could swim in but not get out again. Once set up, a fish trap needed checking only once a day, allowing energy-efficient exploitation of aquatic food resources.

Left: Emmer wheat. This wild form of wheat was a staple food of the Natufian sedentary hunter-gatherers of the Levant at the end of the Ice Age. It was hunter-gatherer societies like the Natufians that first made the transition from simply harvesting wild cereals to cultivating them.

barley, almond, oak, and pistachio trees. These abundant supplies of easily stored cereal and nut foods allowed the Natufian hunter-gatherers to settle permanently in villages of substantial stone and wood huts. As in Scandinavia, there were also temporary camps away from the main settlement that were used for short periods to exploit seasonally abundant resources. The Natufians developed all sorts of specialized tools for processing these tooth-cracking plant foods, including querns, grindstones, mortars and pestles, stone storage bowls, and bone-handled reaping knives for harvesting cereals. Though heavily dependent on plant foods, the Natufians also hunted gazelle in large numbers. Natufian cemeteries have yielded clear evidence of a class system as there are wide variations in the range and quality of grave goods found in individual

burials. Dentalium seashells, a prized item of jewelry across the Near East (as well as North America), are found in some burials but not in others, suggesting that many Natufians lacked the means to obtain them. Wealth or status may have been inherited as a minority of child burials had elaborate grave goods, while a majority had few or none.

Historically, sedentary complex hunter-gatherers are important because it was in this type of community that farming first began as a way of life: their lifestyle and social structures had pre-adapted complex hunter-gatherers for the farming way of life. The Natufians' way of life is of particular significance because it was only a short step for them to move from harvesting wild cereals to planting them. What made them make this step will be examined in the next chapter.

Above: A mask made from the antlers and skull of a red deer from the Mesolithic site at Star Carr, Yorkshire, England. The mask may have been used as camouflage by a hunter when stalking deer or it may have formed part of a shaman's ritual headdress.

CHAPTER TEN

The First Farmers

Until recently historians and archeologists regarded the discovery of agriculture as an unmixed blessing, one of the great break-throughs of human progress. It was believed that pioneering individuals, like the emperor Shen-Nung of Chinese legend, realized that farming would provide people with a more reliable food supply than could be provided by hunting and gathering and would free them from the threat of starva-tion. Though the importance of the adoption of agriculture for human history can hardly be underestimated – our modern civilization is only made possible by the food surpluses created by farmers – the truth is somewhat more complicated.

We now know that hunter-gatherers did not live constantly with the threat of starva-tion and that they had considerable leisure time to enjoy a rich social and ritual life. Sur-viving skeletal evidence shows that the hunter-gatherers of the Upper Paleolithic were well nourished and lived healthy lives. In contrast, the skeletons of early farmers from all over the world show signs of mal-nutrition and stunted growth, arthritis, and other signs of wear and tear caused by hard manual work, excessive tooth wear, disease, and reduced life expectancy. Early farmers in Greece and Turkey averaged 5 feet 3 inches tall for men, 5 feet 1 inch for women: their Paleolithic hunter-gatherer ancestors had averaged 5 feet 10 inches and 5 feet 6 inches respectively, taller even than the

Right: The polished stone bracelets and simple clay bowls identify this as an early Neolithic female burial. Cys-la-Commune, northern France.

Below: Peace and plenty: Egyptian peasants threshing wheat, *c.*1400 BC. In fact the adoption of agriculture created problems as well as benefits.

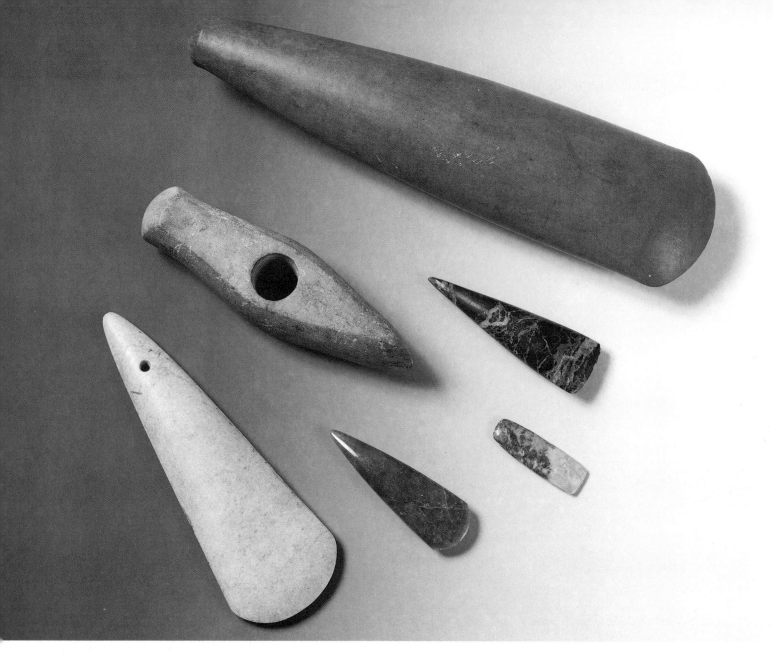

well-nourished modern inhabitants of those countries. After the Indians of the Ohio and Illinois valleys adopted farming *c.*AD 1000 they experienced increased levels of mal-nutrition, tooth decay, and osteoarthritis and, while over 5 percent of the population had lived beyond the age of 50 before the adoption of farming, only 1 percent did so afterwards. Infant mortality also increased.

There were two causes of these problems. The first was the tendency of farmers to rely on a limited range of high-yielding crops. For example, the Mesolithic hunter-gatherers at Tell Abu Hureyra in Syria exploited 150 dif-ferent species of plant foods, the first farmers to inhabit the site used only eight. If one or more of these crops failed due to bad weather, disease, or pests – something which could be expected once every five to eight years on average – the farmers went short of food. The second factor was the increased birth rate of farming societies. The settled farming life meant that women could have more children, and though this meant extra mouths to feed it also meant extra hands to work the land. This

was economically desirable (as it still is in many Third World countries) as it meant in-creased yields most of the time but, in years when the crops failed, it meant that there were too many people to make a return to hunting and gathering a practical alternative. Frequent periods of malnutrition were the in-evitable result. The farmers' health also suffered because infectious diseases were transmitted more easily in the often insanitary conditions of the permanent settlements. Starch-rich diets led to increased tooth decay among farmers and their teeth wore down quickly as a result of eating flour containing grit from grindstones. Women's health may have suffered even more than men's. Women spent hours a day bent over grindstones and querns, processing grain, making them vul-nerable to osteoarthritis of the lower back: in-creased childbearing also took its toll. Early farmers also had to spend an average of 50-100 percent more time working than hunter-gatherers and the work was usually physically more demanding too.

With all these disadvantages, why did

Above: Polished stone axes and a mace head. Though very time-consuming to make, polished stone tools were more durable than those made of chipped stone and were easily resharpened. The three smaller axes, made of exotic stone, were probably made for gift exchange and display rather than serious use. Brittany, 3000-2000 BC.

people abandon hunting and gathering for farming? The short answer is that they had no choice in the matter. The more intensive methods of exploiting natural resources that had come into use in the Mesolithic, together with the more sedentary lifestyle this allowed, seems to have led to a slight relaxation of the tight controls most hunter-gatherers exercised over fertility. The slowly rising populations exerted a constant incentive to find still more intensive methods of exploiting food resources. Over-hunting reduced game stocks and the hunter-gatherers were forced to increase their reliance on plant foods. Casually planting the seeds of favored plant foods to ensure the next year's harvest was probably the first step along the road to farming. After this may have come more deliberate planting close to the home base which would have brought a saving in traveling time. Hunter-gatherers would have quickly learned which species best repaid the effort of planting and these would have increased in importance to the diet. Once set on this route, however, hunter-gatherers would have found it increasingly difficult to turn back. The rising population would have progressively outstripped the environment's capacity to feed it, so increasing its dependence on the cultivation of high-yielding plant foods. The time taken for this process varied greatly. In the Oaxaca valley in Mexico, the transition from hunting and gathering to dependence on cultivated foods extended over 6500 years, from 10,000 BP to 3500 BP (8000-1500 BC). On the other hand, at Tell Abu Hureyra in Syria the transition from hunting and gathering to cultivating cereals and herding seems to have taken place in just a couple of generations around 9000 BP (7000 BC).

Agriculture developed quite independently in the Near East, Southeast Asia, China, New Guinea, Mexico, and Peru between 10,000 and 8000 years ago. Farming spread out from the centers, partly through migrations of farming peoples out of areas that were becoming overpopulated and partly through hunter-gatherers adopting the ways of neighboring farming peoples, usually as a result of population pressure on natural resources. Farming spread quickly and by 2000 years ago had supplanted hunting and gathering as the way of life of most of the human race. In the Old World, the period between the beginning of farming and the adoption of metal tools is known as the Neolithic (New Stone Age). From this, the adoption and early spread of farming is often described as the Neolithic Revolution.

Below: Quernstones for grinding flour were an essential item in every Neolithic household. Women had to spend several hours each day grinding grain for bread or porridge. The repetitive movements made women prone to arthritis in the lower back as early as their twenties.

The earliest communities to rely on farming for most of their food developed in an area of the Near East known as the Fertile Crescent. This is an area of good soils and light but reliable rainfall which extends in an arc from the foothills of Iraq's Zagros Mountains, through southern Turkey to Syria and Israel. The rich resources of wild cereals and other plants allowed sedentary hunter-gatherers like the Natufians to flourish in the last millennia of the Ice Age. Around 10,500 years ago the climate of the region became drier and less favorable to the growth of wild cereals. Cereals continued to grow on higher ground where there was more rainfall, but the Natufians had to live in the valleys, close to the fresh water sources. Not only was the food supply reduced, it was also inconveniently placed. The solution to the problem was to bring the food and the water together by starting to cultivate wild cereals close to the settlements. Other communities in the region, faced with similar problems, came to similar solutions.

Cultivation of wild plants, known as incipient agriculture, is only the beginning of the adoption of a farming way of life. The next stage is the domestication of wild plants

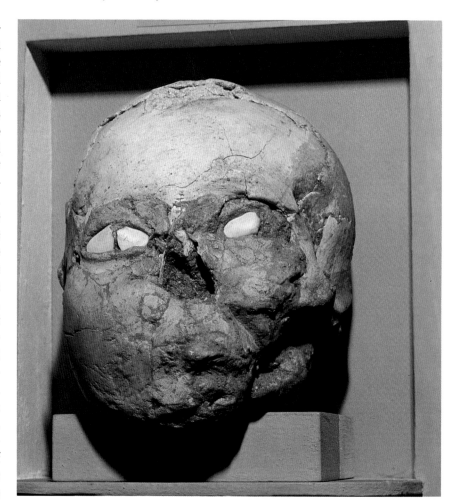

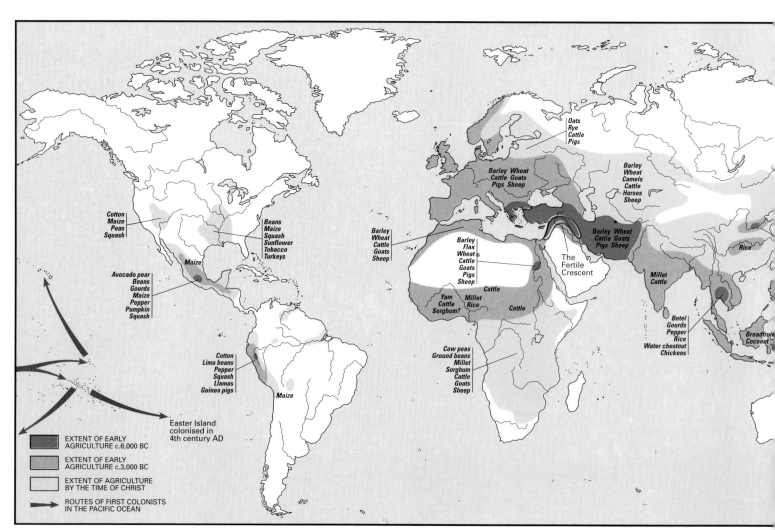

Left: Skull from Jericho with features modeled in clay with shell eyes, *c.*6000 BC. Burial customs became more complex as ancestors came to symbolize an early farming community's ownership of its land.

Right: Defensive walls and tower of early Neolithic Jericho, *c.*7000 BC. The defenses were probably built to protect the farming settlement against desert nomads or other farming communities envious of Jericho's reliable water supply.

Below: The spread of agriculture around the world. Agriculture developed independently at many different centers worldwide.

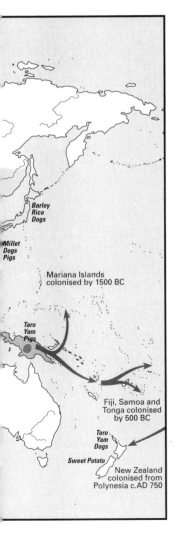

Barley
Rice
Dogs

Millet
Dogs
Pigs

Mariana Islands
colonised by 1500 BC

Taro
Yam
Pigs

Fiji, Samoa and
Tonga colonised
by 500 BC

Taro
Yam
Dogs

Sweet Potato

New Zealand
colonised from
Polynesia c.AD 750

and animals, that is the process of selective breeding which improves their usefulness to humans. For example, wild cereals have small grains and are awkward to harvest because the grains break off the ear and scatter on the ground as soon as they are ripe. However, all animal and plant species contain a certain amount of variability: some individual plants will have had larger than average grains or seedheads that were less prone to scatter when harvested than others. By selectively planting the grains from these plants, early farmers in the Near East were, between 10,000 BP and 9000 BP (8000-7000 BC), able to breed high-yielding strains of cereals with seedheads which did not scatter when harvested. This selection has gone so far that domesticated wheat and barley are almost wholly dependent on humans to propagate them as they now cannot scatter their own seeds.

The domestication of animals in the Near East began at about the same time as the domestication of plants. Far fewer animals than plants are suitable for domestication. Some, such as deer and gazelle are too nervous, others, including most carnivores, are too aggressive. Carnivores are also unsuit-

able for domestication as they compete with man for precious meat (the dog was an early exception to this rule because of its usefulness in hunting and defense against other predators). Grazing animals like sheep, goats, and cattle, that instinctively follow a leader are the most suitable for domestication as they are easily managed and can convert plants that humans cannot eat into meat and milk. Probably the first stage of domestication was restricting the movement of wild herds, perhaps by penning animals and keeping them alive until they were needed for food. After this came selective breeding for desirable characteristics such as docility. However, perhaps because their grazing was now restricted, most early domesticated animals suffered the same reduction of stature as their human masters and were smaller than their wild counterparts. The extinct European wild cow, the aurochs, stood 6 feet tall at the shoulder compared with 4-5 feet for most breeds of modern cattle: Neolithic domesticated cattle were smaller still. Though this reduced the meat yield, it did at least have the advantage of making the animals easier to manage.

One of the earliest sites at which

Above: By 3000 BC farmers growing strains of Near Eastern cereals had settled Scotland's remote and windswept Orkney Islands. Knap of Howar Neolithic farm, Papa Westray, Orkney, *c.*3000 BC.

Above right: Oxen plowing with an ard, the simplest and earliest form of plow.

Right: The foundations of an early Neolithic round hut at Banpo, Shaanxi, northern China, *c.*6000 BC. The farmers of Banpo practiced a shifting form of slash and burn or "swidden" agriculture. Once the soil was exhausted the village was abandoned as its inhabitants moved to another site. Several years later, when the soil had recovered, the village was reoccupied.

domesticated animals have been identified is Zawi Chemi Shanidar in the Zagros Mountains. Analysis of animal bones from the site show that this was originally a settlement of wild-goat hunters, but around 10,000 BP (8000 BC) sheep bones begin to outnumber those of goats by 16 to one. As 60 percent of the bones came from animals that were one year old or younger, it is clear that it was a carefully managed flock under close human control: if the sheep had been hunted we would expect to find a much more random distribution of ages in the sample. Plants and animals were not always domesticated at the same time: in the western part of the Fertile Crescent, plants were domesticated before animals but in the east, as at Zawi Chemi Shanidar, it was the other way around.

Farming spread out from the Fertile Crescent eastward across the Iranian plateau and into the Indus valley. A site at Mehrgarh in Pakistan has shown that farming based on wheat, barley, dates, sheep, and goats was well established in the region by 8000 BP (6000 BC). Mehrgarh has also provided the earliest evidence for the domestication of

cotton and the Indian wild cow or zebu. Farming also spread quickly from the Fertile Crescent through Anatolia and into Greece, the Balkans, Italy, and Spain by 8000 BP.

The first farming culture of temperate Europe is known as the Bandkeramik (i.e. Linear Pottery), after its distinctively patterned pottery. The Bandkeramik people originated in the northern Balkans c.7300 BP (5300 BC) and began to spread steadily northwest along the belt of fertile loess soils which extends across central Europe from Romania to the Rhineland. There was no mass migration of peoples involved in this process: once the population of a village became too large, a daughter settlement would simply be established a few miles away. The Bandkeramik people did not displace the indigenous Mesolithic hunter-gatherer bands but settled on vacant lands between them, usually near rivers. However, the steady encroachment of the Bandkeramik people must have placed pressure on the hunter-gatherers' resources and they were slowly forced to take up farming themselves and over the course of a few centuries the two populations became assimilated. By the time

Above: Simply decorated Neolithic pottery vessels from Brittany. As it is too heavy and fragile to be much use to hunter-gatherers, the presence of pottery on a site is usually a sign of the adoption of a sedentary farming lifestyle.

Left: Late Neolithic Beaker culture burial from southern Britain, *c.*2000 BC. The individual burials of this culture, which are always accompanied by a beaker-shaped drinking pot, show a change to a less communal form of society than that of the early Neolithic.

the Bandkeramik culture ended *c.*6500 BP (4500 BC) most of central Europe was occupied by farmers. Over the following thousand years farming spread across the northern European plain into Russia, southern Scandinavia, France, and Britain. By 5500 BP (3500 BC) there were even farming communities in the remote Orkney and Shetland islands off Scotland's northern coast.

The spread of farming into temperate Europe was made possible by the development of new strains of wheat and barley which were adapted to the cooler climate. The northern Europeans also domesticated the indigenous wild oat, which was more resistant to damp and cold than wheat and barley, and the aurochs and wild pig, both of which were better suited to grazing and foraging in the region's dense forests than sheep and goats.

Farming in Southeast Asia began about 8000 years ago, probably in southern Thailand. Southeast Asia was rich in high-yielding carbohydrate root crops, such as yams and taro, that readily lent themselves to cultivation. Yams and taro can be propagated easily from tubers or cuttings, all that is needed is a small clearing to plant them in. Farming may have begun as early as 9000 years ago in New Guinea. The first plant to be cultivated was probably the indigenous sweet potato but from 6000 years ago this was supplemented by yams and taro which were probably introduced from Southeast

Asia. The spur to adopt agriculture in Southeast Asia and New Guinea was probably the rapidly rising post-glacial sea level which inundated huge areas of low-lying plains, greatly restricting the resources of the indigenous hunter-gatherers. Increasingly dense forest cover must also have increased the pressures to begin food production.

Farming in northern Thailand, Burma, and India's Ganges plain began with the domestication of rice sometime before 9000 BP (8000 BC). By 7000 BP (5000 BC) rice had been adopted in the Yangtze valley in China

Below: Neolithic polished stone ax in an antler socket and a reconstructed wooden haft. Such axes were essential for clearing farmland of trees and scrub.

from where it spread to Korea (*c*.3500 BP/1500 BC) and Japan (*c*.2300 BP/300 BC). Unlike yams and taro, rice is a very labor-intensive crop, but has a higher yield than any other cereal except maize. Rice needs a constant supply of fresh water if it is to grow well, so cultivation probably began on flood plains, but by 6000 years ago farmers in the Yangtze valley had learned to build the terraced paddy fields which are such a typical feature of the Southeast Asian landscape.

Northern China was too dry for rice cultivation but had fertile loess soils which could be easily worked with simple tools like hoes. The most important wild cereal here was millet and this had been domesticated by 8000 BP in the Yellow River valley. However, millet is deficient in important proteins and amino acids and the early farmers of northern China were frail-boned and around a foot shorter on average than their hunter-gatherer predecessors. Only with the domestication of the soya bean, around 4500 years ago, were these nutritional deficiencies remedied.

The earliest center of agriculture in Africa was, surprisingly, the eastern Sahara. At the end of the Ice Age, the Sahara had a much higher rainfall than it has today; there were extensive grasslands which included wild strains of wheat and barley which had been domesticated by 9000 years ago. Sheep, goats, and cattle, presumably introduced from the Near East were also herded. About 7000 years ago the Saharan climate became hotter and drier and desertification began.

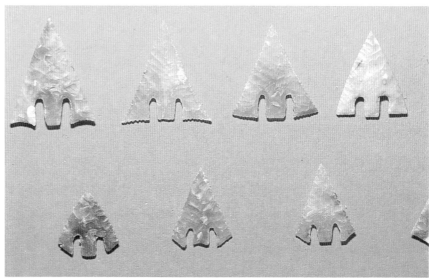

Below left: Flint hoe blade, Temple Mound culture, Mississippi valley, *c.*AD 1200. In farming communities which did not adopt the plow, the hoe remained the most important agricultural implement.

Left: Pot with vigorous bird decoration. Burial Mound culture, Mississippi Valley, *c.*500 BC–AD 500.

Some farmers retreated eastward into the narrow but fertile Nile valley, others moved south to the edges of the West African rain-forests, where, around 6500 years ago they domesticated indigenous strains of millet, sorghum, and yams.

In the Americas the transition from hunt-ing and gathering to a full farming way of life was a much more hesitant and drawn-out affair than it was in Eurasia. The earliest evi-dence of farming in the Americas comes from Guitarrero Cave in the Peruvian Andes. The Andes have a wide range of habitats and by 11,000 BP (9000 BC) they sup-ported a dense population of hunter-gatherers. Population pressure soon led these hunter-gatherers to experiment with food production and as early as 10,500 BP, protein-rich beans had been domesticated. Within a few centuries, gourds and potatoes were also being cultivated in the Andes. However, the Andeans continued to rely on hunting and gathering for most of their food for another 5-6000 years, by which time the llama and guinea pig had been domesticated and maize and beans had been introduced to the region from Mesoamerica. Farming in the Amazon basin began with the domesti-cation of manioc, sweet potato, yams, and peanuts around 8000 years ago and then spread very slowly through the rainforest areas, mainly along rivers.

The other center for the development of agriculture in the Americas was in the Oaxaca and Tehuacan valleys of Mexico. As in the Andes, limited cultivation may have begun around 10,000 years ago but it was less than 4000 years ago that the Mesoamer-icans came to depend on farming for most of their food. The Mesoamericans had a good source of vegetable protein in the kidney bean but the lack of a suitable high-yielding, carbohydrate-rich crop was a major restraint on the development of farming. The main wild cereal of the region is teosinte, the wild ancestor of maize. This had been domesti-cated by 7000 years ago but its cobs were still only 1-2 inches long, compared to 6-9 inches for modern maize. It took another 3500 years of selective breeding before the cobs were large enough to make maize the staple crop of the Americas.

In North America, limited cultivation of seed-bearing plants such as sunflowers had begun by around 4500 years ago in the Illinois and Mississippi basins. However, the transition to a full farming way of life was not possible until the introduction of maize and beans from Mesoamerica late in the first millennium BC. By AD 1000 farming was widespread in southwestern and east-ern North America and was beginning to spread into the Great Plains by the time of the first European contacts.

Center left: Neolithic flint arrowheads, Wales. Hunting continued to make an important contribution to the food supply of many Neolithic communities.

Below center: The plow and wheeled vehicles were not adopted in the Americas because of the lack of suitable draft animals. The llama is a hardy pack animal but it cannot be yoked to a plow or a cart.

Below right: Tassili rock paintings of cattle in the Sahara, 6000-4000 BC. The Sahara has not always been a desert: c.9000 years ago it was home to Africa's first farming communities.

CHAPTER ELEVEN

Tribes and Chiefdoms: Early Farming Societies

The adoption of farming led to revolutionary social and technological changes and involved humans in a completely new relationship with the environment. Hunter-gatherers make little impact on the environment. Some, like the Australian Aborigines, have a superficial impact through the use of simple woodland management techniques, such as controlled burning, to stimulate new growth to improve grazing and attract game. Over-hunting at the end of the Ice Age played a part in the extinction of many species of large mammals, but most hunter-gatherer societies evolved value systems which helped to limit their environmental impact. Apart from scatterings of stone tools and bones, plus a few cave paintings, Paleolithic and Mesolithic hunter-gatherers have left no trace of their passing. With the adoption of agriculture this changed as humans began actively to adapt the natural environment to their economic, social, and cultural needs. Forests were felled, watercourses diverted, cultivation terraces and field boundaries constructed. The farmers' sedentary lifestyle meant that it was worth their while to invest time and effort in building durable houses, stores, workshops, defenses, and

Below: Interior of a Neolithic house, Skara Brae, Orkney, *c.*3000 BC. Permanently settled farmers built much more substantial dwellings than their nomadic hunter-gatherer ancestors.

Left: Foundations of mud-brick houses at Çatal Hüyük Neolithic village, Turkey. *c.*7000 BC. The farming way of life allowed large concentrations of people to live together for the first time. One of the largest known Neolithic settlements, Çatal Hüyük had a population of several thousands.

ritual structures of timber, stone, earth, or sun-baked mud-bricks. These have left substantial archeological remains, which even after millennia of weathering and erosion can still leave us awestruck.

Farmers spent much of their time working and socializing in their houses, so it was also worth their while to invest time and effort to make them comfortable and attractive. In the Neolithic village at Skara Brae in Scotland's Orkney Islands, houses had stone cupboards and sleeping shelves, hearths, cooking pits, and drains. The prestige value of having a bigger house than one's neighbors was also soon realized. In the Near East multi-roomed, multi-storied houses were already being built as status symbols 9000 years ago. Interior decoration also goes back a long way: interior walls in the houses at the 9000-year-old Anatolian village of Çatal Hüyük were painted to brighten them up. Architecture, the quest to create the ideal home and keeping one step ahead of the neighbors all began with the Neolithic.

The first farmers not only began to change the appearance of the environment, they sometimes damaged it permanently. The problems caused by deforestation, overgrazing, soil exhaustion, and poor irrigation techniques often make headlines today, but they are almost as old as agriculture itself: as long as 8000 years ago villages in Jordan were being abandoned because of soil erosion and desertification caused by deforestation. Farming also introduced a new con-

frontational element into human relations with nature. Wild plants which competed with crops for light and nutrients were weeded out; animals like wolves and foxes which preyed on flocks and herds were hunted down with the intention of making them extinct – an activity completely alien to the hunter-gatherer mentality. Nevertheless, early farmers remained close to nature as is clear from their religious beliefs which were usually linked to the passing of the seasons and cycles of life, death, and renewal.

Farmers needed a different technology to hunter-gatherers and because they were

Below: Polished stone battle axes, Finland, *c.*1800 BC. Because of the time taken to make them, polished stone tools and weapons were important prestige objects in early farming societies.

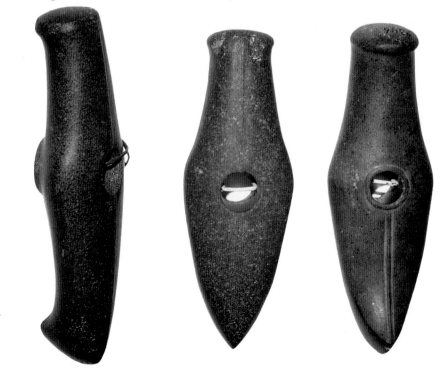

sedentary they were not restricted to making artifacts which were easily portable. Though both are also used by some sedentary hunter-gatherers, the two types of artifact which are most typical of early farming communities are those made of polished stone and pottery. Early farmers the world over needed heavy axes and adzes to clear forests and for woodworking, but chipped stone tools fractured too easily for this kind of work. Polished stone tools were far more efficient and durable and it was well worth a farmer's while to take the extra time and effort needed to make them. Experiments with modern replicas of polished stone tools have shown that, though they needed frequent resharpening, they compared well with early metal tools. Hunter-gatherers in the Paleolithic knew that fire could be used to harden clay, but pottery was heavy and fragile so very little practical use was made of the knowledge. Farmers had much more need of storage vessels and cooking pots than hunter-gatherers and, as they did not have to carry them very far, weight and fragility were no longer obstacles to the widespread adoption of pottery.

Farmers also needed the means to break the ground before planting. The stone hoe was the most universally used ground-breaking tool but in Eurasia the plow began to replace it after c.6000 BC (the plow was never adopted in the Americas and many parts of Africa and Asia because of the lack of suitable draft animals). Neolithic farmers in Eurasia developed a wide range of simple machines – levers and rollers for moving heavy objects, the wheel (first used for throwing pottery), the sail, and the loom for weaving animal and plant fibers – and, discovered how to smelt metal ores and cast artifacts in gold, silver, lead, and copper. These technological innovations became the mainstays of the first Old World civilizations. Technological development in the New World was more limited: the only metals worked were gold, silver, and copper, all of which occur naturally in the native form, and the wheel never came into use either for transport or making pottery.

The smaller territories and increasingly specialized needs of farmers meant that their communities were often less self-sufficient than hunter-gatherer bands. As a result, gift exchanges and trade became more important. Food must have been an important object of exchange as all communities will have suffered shortages at some time but,

Right: Reconstruction of an ancient Egyptian potter's wheel. The invention of the potter's wheel in the Near East c.4000 BC accelerated pottery production and allowed a wider variety of shapes to be made.

Below right: Traditional weaving methods, Yemen. This type of loom has been in use for around 6000 years: though simple it can produce complex patterns and high-quality cloth.

Below: A human sacrificial victim is drowned in a ritual vessel in this scene from the Gundestrup Cauldron, Denmark, c.200-150 BC. Chiefdoms were the first societies in which leaders enjoyed real coercive powers, including that of life and death.

being perishable, traces of this kind of trade are rare. However, Neolithic farmers in the Fertile Crescent do appear to have traded grain for animal products with neighboring hunter-gatherers. Top quality stone for tool-making was traded over long distances. Obsidian (volcanic glass) from El Chayel in Guatemala was traded over distances of 400 miles or more. In the British Isles polished stone axes were traded over hundreds of miles, some have been found made of rock which occurs only in the Italian Alps. Luxu-ries were also traded over long distances: lapis lazuli from Afghanistan was traded as far away as Egypt in the Neolithic. Once metal tools came into widespread use in Eurasia, these long distance contacts be-came even more important. Trade was mostly small scale and there were probably no full-time merchants in the Neolithic. However, at least 9000 years ago a preco-cious settlement of several thousand people at Çatal Hüyük in Turkey flourished on a mixture of farming and trading in high-quality obsidian from nearby quarries.

The agricultural way of life can support far greater population densities than can hunt-ing and gathering. Even in a favorable en-vironment, a single hunter-gatherer may need 10 square miles to make a living. In contrast, the simplest form of "slash-and-burn" agriculture (a system which involves making a clearing and cultivating it for a few years until soil fertility declines and forces a move to another site) can support over 50

people per square mile: a potential 50,000 percent population increase. Agriculture therefore made possible a vast increase in the human population, even if this was sometimes at the expense of the health and life expectancy of the individual farmer. Moreover, there was now an incentive to have as many children as possible: the bigger the labor force, the more land could be cultivated, the more care could be taken of it and the bigger the yield would be.

Farmers could also increase the productiv-ity of their land by adopting new tech-nology, new crops, and new practices such as manuring and crop rotation. A good example of this is the development of the

Above: Mother goddesses from Çatal Hüyük. Mother goddesses are a common feature of the religious art of many early farming societies, probably because of their natural interest in fertility.

Right: Mud-brick manufacture near Cairo. Since the Neolithic, mud-brick has been an important building material in areas of low rainfall such as the Near East. The mud is mixed with straw to bind it, shaped in a mold and simply left to dry in the sun. In wetter climates bricks must be baked if they are not to dissolve in rainwater.

Left: Mareb, Yemen. In the Near East, farming settlements have occupied the same sites for many thousands of years. The accumulation of domestic refuse and debris from mud-brick houses has built up mounds, known as "tells," which can be up to 100 feet high.

Left: The Sun Chariot from Trundholm Bog, Sjaelland, Denmark, *c.*1000 BC. Chiefdoms were able to support specialist craftworkers capable of producing superb works of art.

Right: Bronze Age burial of a man in an oak coffin, Denmark, 1500-800 BC. The bronze shield and dagger mark this man out as a high status member of a warrior class.

Below: A small Neolithic passage grave, Mons, Denmark. This communal tomb is rather more typical of megalithic monuments than great works like Stonehenge or Newgrange.

tools used to prepare the soil for planting. The earliest farmers simply used digging sticks to make a hole and drop a seed into it, but most farming societies quickly adopted the stone-bladed hoe for breaking up the surface of the soil. The invention of the plow in the Near East around 6000 years ago made possible a further advance in productivity. The first plows were sharpened or stone-tipped sticks that were dragged across the soil by asses or oxen. This type of plow, known as an ard, could break the surface of the soil with much less effort than using a hoe. The ard was gradually refined and after the discovery of metalworking its cutting point was reinforced with a metal blade, enabling it to cut deeper and faster. An even greater improvement came with the separate invention of the moldboard plow in China and Europe in the first millennium AD which, with its curved share, could cut deep and turn the soil, improving its fertility, suppressing weed growth, and greatly increasing yields. The effect of every improvement of the plow was to increase the acreage that could be effectively worked by one man; the greatest increases coming with mechanization in this present century. In areas of low rainfall, the use of irrigation brought similar increases in productivity.

Most farmers, most of the time, were able to produce more food than they and their families needed. This surplus food – the earliest form of wealth – had a dramatic effect

on the structure of human societies. Surplus food could be exchanged for other goods and services or be used to buy popularity and influence. As people could use their surpluses to improve their standard of living and status they became unwilling to share it outside the immediate family. Some people worked harder than others, some had more fertile soil to cultivate, so differences of wealth and poverty began to emerge in early farming societies. Because more people could now live off less land, farming made it possible for people to live together in larger groups.

The earliest farming societies were similar in structure to complex hunter-gatherers in resource-rich environments. The basic unit was the tribe, a kinship-based unit, usually numbering around 100 strong. Tribes remained fairly egalitarian societies which probably held land in communal ownership. However, ambitious individuals or "Big Men" could use accumulated food surpluses to win prestige and influence through the "potlatch" system of competitive feasting (see chapter nine), leading to disparities of wealth and status. Big Men stimulated the production of prestige objects such as finely decorated pottery, jewelry, and polished stone tools and weapons which were displayed at feasts and handed out as gifts. Competitive feasting and gift exchange played an important role in relationships between tribes, cementing alliances but also causing wars if one tribe felt it was being shortchanged by another. In New Guinea, where this kind of society still exists, warfare was endemic but its destructive effects were limited by universally observed rituals and conventions: only rarely are lands seized and populations wiped out. However, the rock-cut ditch and masonry walls and towers built 10,000 years ago by the inhabitants of Jericho suggest that warfare of a more serious nature was prevalent in some areas right from the start of the Neolithic.

One of the best archeological examples of a Neolithic community at the "Big Man" stage of development is Çayönü in Turkey. The center of this village was a 1000 square yard plaza. This could be identified as a communal open-air feasting area, such as are still found in New Guinea, from fragments of high-quality pottery and other prestige goods which were found toward the edges of the plaza. Prestige goods were displayed here to impress the guests at feasts; some inevitably got broken and the remains got swept or kicked to the edge of the plaza, out of the way. The plan of the village and the contents of its houses both show that there were differences in wealth and status among the inhabitants of Çayönü. The houses which were built adjacent to the plaza were on average almost twice the size of any others in the village and much better built. Some may have been two stories high. The plaza houses contained high status goods – obsidian blocks, sculptures, rare seashells, copper beads, semi-precious stones, and polished stone tools – which were rarely found in the smaller houses. Another sign of social ranking in the village is that though many houses contained burials, only those found in the plaza houses contained grave goods.

Tribal societies tolerated Big Men but they had little real power: if a Big Man got too pushy, the rest of the tribe could simply ignore him. Nor are the resources available

Left: Medicine man of the Huli tribe, Papua New Guinea, with the skulls of his forebears. The study of Papua New Guinea's still surviving Stone Age farmers has given many insights into the structures of Neolithic tribal societies.

Below: Chiefdoms were competitive and warlike societies which expended considerable resources on building defenses. This hill-top village site at Tre'r Ceiri, North Wales, was defended by a double circuit of stone walls which can still be clearly seen over 2000 years after they were built.

to a Big Man so great that he and his family do not have to work on their own land. However, in societies which had abundant resources some Big Men achieved real power, including that of life and death, over their fellows as hereditary chieftains. Chiefdoms grew out of loose tribal alliances and have much larger populations than tribes, 1000 being about the minimum viable population while numbers in excess of 20,000 are not unusual. Archeologists can recognize chiefdoms by the presence of large monuments, prestige burials, human sacrifices, craft specialization, and other evidence of the existence of centralized power and hierarchical social structure such as the presence of a hierarchy of places. Settlements of farming societies in the "Big Man" stage of development are all very much the same size, but in chiefdoms there is often one settlement which is

very much larger than those surrounding it. This can be seen clearly in the area around Danebury in southern England, where an Iron Age hillfort – the headquarters of the chiefdom – is surrounded by smaller dependent farming villages.

Archeologists are still far from certain how chieftains managed to acquire coercive power. One possibility is that Big Men exploited the skills gained through organizing competitive feasts to gain control over the accumulation and distribution of food surpluses. Particularly in times of shortage, this would give the Big Man great coercive power. This may have been a particularly important factor in areas of dense population where many people would have eked out a precarious existence on unproductive marginal land. Another possibility is that Big Men achieved a monopoly in the distribution of

essential trade goods such as stone or salt (the plant foods on which most early farmers depended were deficient in salt) and threatened to end supplies to those who refused obedience. In farming societies which used metal tools and weapons, whoever controlled the distribution of metal enjoyed not only coercive economic power but also coercive military power. In areas such as Mesopotamia where irrigation was essential for agriculture, Big Men may have used control over water resources to gain power.

Once they had gained their power, the chieftains set themselves apart from their subjects in various ways. Myth and religion were used to give the chief a sacred aura, as with the Polynesian chiefs who could place persons and things under "taboo." A chief might claim a common ancestry for himself and all the people of the tribe and proclaim himself

the senior member of this fictive extended family with a right to exercise a father's authority over it. This kind of fictive kinship was an important feature of the Gaelic clans of Ireland and Highland Scotland until as late as the eighteenth century AD. Cults of ancestor worship legitimized hereditary succession to the chieftaincy. Burial practices were also designed to reinforce the succession. The dead chief would be accompanied by prestige goods such as fine pottery, jewelry and weapons, food, and, the ultimate expression of power, human sacrifices. These offerings may have been intended to secure the chief's place in the afterlife but they were also a dramatic demonstration of the wealth and power of his successor. Now that they could order someone else to do it for them, chiefs no longer had to do manual work. Some chiefs deliberately emphasized this privilege by

Above: The Newgrange passage grave, Co. Meath, Ireland, *c.*3200 BC. This huge tomb could only have been built by a powerful chiefdom able to command resources over a wide area. Unlike earlier megalithic monuments which were communal tombs, Newgrange was built as a burial place for a chiefly elite. The tomb was so aligned that at sunrise on the winter solstice the sun could shine, briefly, directly into the burial chamber.

impractical affectations: for example, the Maya chiefs grew their fingernails very long and overate to the point of obesity. Chiefs also demonstrated their status by wearing expensive jewelery, special clothes, or even tattoos. Certain valuable items might be reserved only for the chief's use.

Chiefdoms did not possess police forces and standing armies so there were severe limits on the chief's power. If a chief could not enforce his power over his people, why did they accept his power over them? Why did people not simply overthrow the chief and help themselves to his wealth as soon as he used his economic power to demand obedience? The answer must be that most people saw it as being in their interest to obey. The chief's stored food and other wealth could be used in all sorts of ways that benefited, however unequally, all members of society. Those tribal leaders and Big Men who lost their independence by acknowledging a chief could expect to be rewarded for their support, and they would enjoy secure aristocratic status within the hierarchy of the chiefdom – a definite gain as the status of a Big Man is always insecure. Food could be redistributed in times of famine to provide a safety net against starvation: it could be traded for essential imports and desirable luxuries; it could be used to feed people while they worked on irrigation canals, dams, cultivation terraces, or defenses in which the whole community had an interest or on prestige projects, such as building a megalithic monument, to enhance the chief's image. Chiefs who did not deliver benefits to their people were often overthrown, taboos and traditions notwithstanding.

Because the power of the chief is insecure, chiefdoms are highly competitive societies. A chief must always try to increase the resources at his disposal to reward his followers, whether peacefully, through agricultural improvements, or by violent plunder and conquest. The increased importance of warfare led to the emergence of elite warrior classes in many chiefdoms, such as among the Maya and Olmec of Mesoamerica or the Celts of Bronze and Iron Age Europe. Defensive refuges, often built on commanding hilltops or other defensible positions, are also common features of chiefdoms in all parts of the world. Competition also manifested itself in non-violent ways. Chiefdoms had sufficient resources to support small numbers of highly skilled craftsmen to work

Above: Stonehenge, possibly the most famous of all prehistoric monuments. Stonehenge is a complex site which was gradually modified and added to over a period of 1400 years before it finally fell out of use *c*.1500 BC. The great trilithons – the "hanging stones" – which dominate the site today were erected *c*.2120 BC using no machinery other than simple levers despite their 50-ton weight. The circle was aligned on the midsummer sunrise and may have been a center for seasonal rituals.

full time at producing jewelry, tableware, weapons, armor, and other lavish display objects in semi-precious stone, pottery, and metals. Chiefs could also show off their wealth and power by commissioning major building projects such as the megalithic tombs and stone circles of western Europe. Some megalithic monuments, such as the passage grave at Newgrange in Ireland, built c.3200 BC, and the great stone circle at Stonehenge in England, completed c.2100 BC, were built on a truly massive scale and could only have been completed by very powerful chiefdoms with populations numbering in the tens of thousands. The final stage of the construction of Stonehenge alone required an estimated 30 million man hours of labor to complete.

Competition made chiefdoms very unstable and liable to collapse. An extreme example of this occurred on Easter Island. There chiefdoms competed so intensely with one another to raise ever more ''moai'' (the megalithic stone heads for which the island is famous) that in the end the island's environment was irreparably damaged by deforestation and over-cultivation. Warfare and starvation caused the population to collapse from around 7000 in the sixteenth century AD to only 3000 at the time of the first European landing on Easter Island in 1722.

Despite their sometimes spectacular achievements, chiefdoms are neither states nor civilizations. Chiefdoms lack the centralized administrative institutions and urban communities which are characteristic of civilized state societies. However, given the right circumstances, chiefdoms do have the potential to develop into civilized states. What these circumstances were and where and when they occurred are the subjects of the next two chapters.

Left: A moai on Easter Island. Unrestrained competition between the island's chiefdoms to see which could erect the greatest number of these monumental 20-feet tall, 50-ton, stone carvings led to catastrophic environmental degradation and depopulation.

CHAPTER TWELVE
Sumer: The First Civilization

Generations of historians have agreed that the emergence of civilization was one of the major events of human history, but what exactly do we mean by "civilization?" As it is commonly used, the word civilization implies "civility" and "civilized" values. As a result many of us, if asked to define civilization, would stress the moral qualities shown by a society. Though such an approach might seem simply common sense, such definitions too often turn out to be ethnocentric value judgments: what constitutes civilized behavior in one culture may seem anti-social and barbaric to another. Modern historians have therefore tried to define civilization in terms which avoid value judgments by stressing the complexity of the organizational aspects of society. Though there is still no universally agreed definition, the 10 characteristics proposed by the British prehistorian Gordon Childe have gained widespread support. Childe's work has been refined by the American archeologist Charles Redman, who has subdivided the characteristics into primary and secondary features:

Primary	Secondary
1. settlement in cities	6. monumental public works
2. full-time specialization of labor	7. long-distance trade
3. concentration of surpluses	8. standardized monumental artwork
4. class structure	9. writing
5. state organization	10. arithmetic, geometry, and astronomy

The primary characteristics are all aspects of social organization. The secondary characteristics are aspects of material culture which can be recognized from archeological remains and which point to the existence of some, or all, of the primary features. For example, monumental public works are evidence of a powerful central government and state organization. This list of characteristics,

devoid of value judgments, can be readily applied to any society. We would not expect a generalized hunter-gatherer society to display more than one of the characteristics, while tribally organized complex hunter-gatherers and farmers might show two to four: a chiefdom is a much more complex type of society but will still only display up to three of the secondary and only two or

Below: A votive statue of a woman worshipper from Early Dynastic Sumeria, *c.*3000-2300 BC. These temple statues symbolize the devotion of the donor and give an accurate idea of the appearance of the people of the first civilized society.

three of the primary characteristics. A civilized society will display nearly all of the characteristics – the Incas, for example, had all five primary and four of the secondary characteristics (they could not write) – and most civilizations will display all of them.

Archeologists and historians have proposed many theories to explain the emergence of civilization. Some explanations can be dismissed readily. Civilization did not occur because of any physical or mental changes in humans themselves. Physically and mentally modern humans had evolved by 40-50,000 years ago and there have been only slight superficial changes since then. The first civilizations were therefore created by people who were no different from their Neolithic and Upper Paleolithic ancestors (or from us, for that matter). Technological changes, perhaps surprisingly, also seem to have had little to do with the emergence of civilization. Most of the technology which the first Old World civilizations depended on had been developed hundreds, if not

thousands of years earlier in the Neolithic. Even such advanced techniques as the lost-wax method of bronze casting and iron working were not the exclusive preserve of civilized societies.

The civilizations of the Americas were based on even simpler technologies: they did not even use the wheel or make metal tools. Far more important was the change in subsistence strategy from hunting and gathering to farming, which allowed both population increases and the accumulation of surpluses. However, the simple methods used by the earliest farmers were not productive enough to support the numbers of non-food producers associated with civilized states: these required the intensification of farming techniques. Irrigation and the development and refinement of the plow are the two most important methods by which this could be achieved but there are other ways. Introducing new crops which could be grown on land which was previously unsuitable for agriculture was one. For

Above: One of the great rivers of Mesopotamia, the Euphrates, from an Assyrian frieze, *c.*700 BC. The rivers of Mesopotamia were more than just a source of water for crops and date palms, they were major transport routes and a source of fish. Many early civilizations developed on the flood plains of great rivers where irrigation made intensive agriculture possible.

example, in the Mediterranean region growing olives and vines on rough hillsides which could not support cereals greatly increased productivity. The productivity of animals could also be intensified by exploiting them for milk and wool as well as meat. However, intensification of farming was not the exclusive preserve of civilizations so this alone cannot have caused their emergence.

One of the most influential theories of the emergence of civilization is the so-called "hydraulic theory." The earliest civilizations of the Old World – Mesopotamia, Egypt, and the Indus valley – all developed on the flood plains of great rivers. Though the soils were extremely fertile, rainfall in these areas was so low that farming was only possible with the aid of irrigation. Large-scale irrigation systems required advanced organizational skills to build, maintain, and regulate. These could only be supplied by a centralized body which gained great power from its control over water supplies and used this to establish its authority in other fields of life. The huge increases in production made possible by irrigation enabled the central authority to support large numbers of specialist craftsmen and the administrators needed to regulate the collection and distribution of food surpluses.

Population pressure is seen as a major factor in some theories. As populations expanded, they suggest, the kinship links which formed the basis of tribes and chieftaincies became too attenuated to hold large communities together, forcing the development of more complex social structures. In areas of dense population where expansion was not possible, groups would be forced to compete for resources. Under these circumstances communities will tend to get larger, the better to defend themselves against attack or to increase their chances of success in attacking others. Tribes would amalgamate into chiefdoms and chiefdoms would amalgamate into states. Successful war leaders may have been able to acquire a wider authority in the community, establishing themselves as a ruling class, while the populations of conquered areas might be absorbed by the victors as a lower class. In this way the hierarchical class structure of a state society would emerge. Even if a military class originally emerged as a response to outside aggression, once established it had the means to maintain its position within its own community by force if necessary.

Marxist historians also claim that class

conflict could have promoted the emergence of a hierarchical state structure. As the distinctions of wealth and poverty that had emerged in early farming societies became wider, the wealthy sought to institutionalize their controlling position and use coercion if necessary to deny the poorer classes equal access to resources. Therefore, according to this theory, the civilized state emerged as a means of maintaining the position of a ruling class.

Trade is another factor which has been seen as playing an important role in the emergence of civilization. This may have been particularly important in Mesopotamia which lacked any natural resources other than its fertile soils. Metals, stone, and building timber all had to be imported and this may have led to the development of a centralized body to organize the procure-

Below: A votive statue of a male worshipper from Early Dynastic period, Sumeria, *c.*2600 BC. The man's woolen skirt identifies him as a high official. The development of a bureaucracy is a sign that society has become so complex that it needs full-time administrators to ensure its smooth running.

Above: One of the grave goods from the Royal Cemetery at Ur, a ram made of gold, silver, and lapis lazuli, *c.*2600-2400 BC.

ment and transport of these goods. This centralized body would have been in a good position gradually to extend its authority into other aspects of daily life in the region.

All of these theories have something to offer to our understanding of how civilizations emerged, but it is unlikely that any one of them alone is a sufficient explanation. It is more likely that civilizations arose through a complex interaction of several, or even all, of the factors identified in these theories. Once a civilization is established, it exerts a powerful influence – through trade, war, and culture – over its pre-civilized neighbors, often accelerating their own development toward civilization. Because of this, civilizations can be divided into "primary" and "secondary" types. Primary civilizations are those which

developed independently of any outside influences: these include the Sumerian, Egyptian, Indus valley, Chinese, Minoan, and Olmec civilizations. Secondary civilizations are those, like Greece, Rome, and the Aztecs, which developed under the influence of other civilizations.

The world's first civilization emerged on the flood plain of the Tigris and Euphrates rivers in Iraq, a land which we still know by its ancient Greek name as Mesopotamia, "the land between the rivers." Though its soils were extremely fertile, southern Mesopotamia was unsuitable for farming because of its low rainfall and it was not until farmers in the foothills of the neighboring Zagros Mountains learned how to irrigate their fields *c.*6000 BC that settlement could begin.

The descendants of these settlers called themselves "the dark-headed people" but they are known to history as the Sumerians after the name given to their lands by Sargon the Great who conquered them c.2334 BC.

Irrigating the Mesopotamian plains required a great deal of muscle power but it was not technically difficult. Because, like the Mississippi, the Tigris and the Euphrates have built high levees, the rivers' beds are actually higher than the surrounding plains. It was, therefore, a relatively simple matter to dig canals from the rivers into the surrounding countryside to irrigate farmland: gravity did the rest of the work. The main problem was that the canals would quickly silt up without constant maintenance and digging out. Flood damage had to be repaired and if, as often happened, the rivers changed course, completely new canals had to be built. It is the consequent need for an efficient central authority to manage these essential tasks, that many historians see as beginning the development of civilization in Mesopotamia. Irrigation coupled with the development of heat-resistant strains of wheat and the use of the plow allowed Mesopotamian farmers to produce large surpluses and the population rose quickly: by 5300 BC the whole of Mesopotamia was densely settled and in the south some very large communities were beginning to develop.

These large communities of the Ubaid culture (c.5900-4300 BC) were all built around large central shrines or temples, suggesting that an elite with priestly authority was emerging which could divert part of the food surplus to the propitiation of the gods. The farmers on the plains were always vulnerable to unpredictable floods or changes in the course of the rivers on whose waters they depended. It must have seemed to the farmers that they were the victims of capricious gods: the most famous of all Sumerian myths is that of the flood which the gods sent to punish the human race simply because its noise disturbed their rest. A priestly elite which was believed to be able to fend off divine anger would easily have established its authority over a population which lived in constant fear of natural disaster. It was probably this priestly elite who organized irrigation works, the collection and distribution of surpluses, and trade. One of the largest Ubaid settlements was Eridu, which had become a town of some 5000 inhabitants by c.4500 BC. At the center of the town was a temple dedicated to the water-god Enki. Offerings of fishbones mixed with ashes were found scattered around the temple's altars. Temples of the Ubaid culture, including that at Eridu, were built on 3-feet tall platforms: over the centuries the temples were rebuilt on ever taller platforms until they grew into the ziggurats that dominated Sumerian and Babylonian cities. Most of the inhabitants of Eridu still worked on the land but there was a community of craftsmen who maintained and beautified the temple. The chieftain-priests of Eridu extended their control over smaller dependent villages in the surrounding countryside which supplied the temple community with food.

Though clearly complex and hierarchical, the communities of the Ubaid were basically chiefdoms (they showed only about six of

Left: The partially restored remains of the ziggurat of Ur, Iraq, *c.*2100-2000 BC. Ziggurats – stepped platforms surmounted by temples – were one of the most typical features of the ancient Mesopotamian civilizations. It was the ziggurat of the god Marduk at Babylon which gave rise to the story of the Tower of Babel.

the ten characteristics listed previously), the breakthrough to civilization and state organization occurred in the following period of Mesopotamian prehistory, known as the Uruk (c.4300-3100 BC) after the site on which the world's first true city developed. The Uruk period saw a remarkable growth in the size of the settlements. While the largest Ubaid settlements had not had populations of more than a few thousand, by the end of the Uruk period there were dozens of Sumerian settlements with populations of 2000-8000, while Uruk itself had a population approaching 50,000.

All the major cities of the Sumerian civilization grew up out of settlements of the Ubaid period and they preserved the same basic pattern in that they were built around temple complexes. The temples were run as households, with the god or goddess as its titular head but with the chief priest, or "en," as its effective ruler. The city, its people, and most of its lands were seen as being the property of the god. Until the middle of the

third millennium BC, the temple was the sole source of authority in Sumerian society. The temple community included farmers, gardeners, laborers, craftsmen, merchants, priests, and administrators together with bakers, brewers, and others who prepared the food rations of the community. The food produced on the land were brought to the temple where it was stored and redistributed to the temple community in the form of rations, which varied according to the status of the individual. Pots made to a standard size were used for measuring out these rations. Food which was not required for rations was stored for use in famine years or exchanged for imported raw materials, the distribution of which was also controlled by the temple. Trade links were wide-ranging. Timber and copper were brought from the Anatolian mountains hundreds of miles to the north of Sumeria; building stone from Arabia; lapis lazuli from Afghanistan. The temple also organized labor for public works, such as building and maintaining

Above: Part of a procession delivering tributes of cattle, sheep, fish, and other provisions: a scene from the "peace" side of the so-called Standard of Ur, c.2600-2400 BC. The figures are of shell set in lapis lazuli and bitumen.

irrigation canals or temples on a larger scale than had previously been possible. One stage alone of the construction of the temple of Anu at Uruk took over 65 million man hours to complete.

The efficient administration of the vast quantities of labor and materials which the temples could marshal was beyond the capacity of unaided human memory. The solution to the problem was the invention of writing. No unique genius invented writing, it was invented independently many times in many different parts of the world and it seems to be a natural product of the human capacity for abstract and symbolic thought: Upper Paleolithic humans were capable of inventing writing but they had no need to. The earliest examples of writing come from Uruk and date to *c*.3300 BC but as it was already a complete system with over 700 signs, development must have begun much earlier than this. The earliest Sumerian signs are pictographs: for example the sign for barley is a simplified picture of an ear of barley. More complex ideas could be expressed by combining signs: the combination of a head and a bowl meant "to eat." The signs were inscribed on wet clay tablets using a rectangular-ended reed stylus. This left wedge-shaped strokes from which the Sumerian script gets its name "cuneiform." Over the next thousand years cuneiform was refined so that the sign could also stand for the phonetic value of the word. If we had this system in English, the sign for "man" could

be used in combination with another sign, say for "age," to make another word: "man-age." Syllable signs were also introduced enabling cuneiform accurately to record all elements of human speech. The needs of administration also drove advances in mathematics and the measurement of time.

The adoption of writing by a community marks the end of its prehistory. Writing allowed people to record their beliefs and

Above: Clay tablet from Kish, Iraq, *c*.3100 BC. The earliest form of writing used in Mesopotamia were simple pictographs where each symbol stood for an object or idea. For example the foot symbol (lower left-hand corner) stands for "to walk."

Above right: Stores list in developed cuneiform script, Babylon, *c*.2400 BC. The pictographic script gradually became more abstract and symbols began to be used to represent phonetic values, not just whole words. Cuneiform gets its name, which means "wedge shaped," from the shape of the stylus strokes.

Left: Clay tablet describing geometrical problems, Babylon, *c*.1800 BC. Mesopotamia, and Babylon in particular, was the birthplace of mathematics.

Left: Sumerian cylinder seal and impression, *c.*2900 BC. Cylinder seals were stone, glass, or metal cylinders carved with a design. When they were rolled in wet clay they formed a continuous design. Cylinder seals were used to seal important documents or storage vessels to indicate authenticity or ownership.

values, mythologies, stories, and history but this did not happen immediately. The clay tablets used by the Sumerians are extremely durable and tens of thousands of them have survived to the present day. For the first thousand years of Sumerian civilization, these tablets were used almost exclusively for bookkeeping: lists, receipts, accounts, labels, and mathematical calculations of rations or other supplies. The Sumerian bureaucracy suffered all the ills associated with modern bureaucracies, for example at Ur the death of a single sheep has been found recorded on clay tablets in triplicate!

The Uruk period also saw the appearance of a new form of official, intentionally propagandist art with standardized representations of chief priests interceding with the temple gods. Art and monumental architecture were now combined to project an impression of the power and authority of the ruling class.

Left: Gold, lapis lazuli, and carnelian headdress and jewelry from the Royal Cemetery of Ur, *c.*2500 BC. This is typical of the ceremonial dress of a female attendant at the court of a Sumerian ruler in the Early Dynastic period. Such attendants might be expected to serve their rulers in the afterlife as well as this life: the bodies of many, presumably sacrificed, have been found in royal tombs.

Sumerian civilization was primarily an organizational and administrative achievement but it also made some technological innovations. The most important of these was the discovery of bronze, an alloy of copper and tin, *c*.3000 BC. Copper had been used for millennia for ornaments and even small tools, but it was far too soft to replace stone tools for most purposes. Bronze was tougher and kept its edge much better than copper and could be resharpened more easily than polished stone. Though metal ores and toolmaking stone alike had to be imported into Mesopotamia, bronze tools had the great advantage that when they wore out or broke they could be melted down and recast. Though wheeled vehicles were probably invented up to a thousand years earlier (probably as an adaptation of the potter's wheel), the Sumerians of the Uruk period were the first who are known to have made extensive use of them for transport.

Sumerian civilization entered a new and troubled phase in the Early Dynastic period (3000-2300 BC). Massive defensive walls were built around the cities, bronze weapons were produced in increasing quantities and war begins to feature prominently as the subject of official art with rulers often being shown

Above: A scene from the "war" side of the Royal Standard of Ur, *c*.2600-2400 BC. The slain body being trampled by the victors is a common feature of Mesopotamian and Egyptian triumphal art. The battle wagon is drawn by asses, horses were not domesticated until *c*.2000 BC.

Left: Diorite statue of a Sumerian ruler, Gudea, priest-king of the city of Lagash, *c*.2100 BC. Gudea was an avid temple builder who brought his people peace and prosperity in an unstable period of Mesopotamian history.

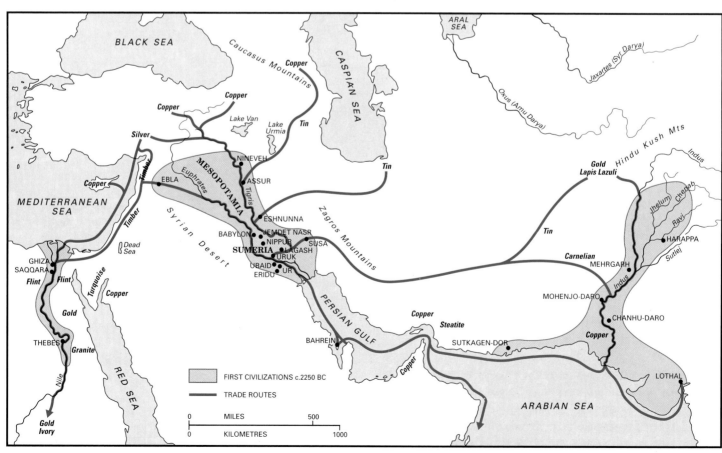

trampling on their enemies. The gap between rich and poor widened and slavery appears in the records for the first time. Secular leaders now appear alongside the ens. Some had the title "sangu," (accountant) suggesting that the bureaucrats had achieved equal status with the priests and others were called "lugal" or "sharru," (king). These last may have been war leaders, elected in times of emergency in the past, who had now made their authority permanent. These secular leaders built palaces next to the temple precincts where they lived in opulence. In death they were given magnificent burials, such as those excavated at the Royal Cemetery of Ur, accompanied by the luxuries of their everyday lives: gold and silver tableware, gold headdresses, jewelry, armor, weapons, statues of gold and lapis lazuli, musical instruments, and, sometimes, even human sacrifices.

Lacking the spiritual authority of the priesthood, the new secular rulers established their authority through law. The earliest surviving law code is that of Urukagina, ruler of Lagash *c.*2350 BC. Urukagina's law code was humane and showed great concern to protect the poor from arbitrary bureaucratic decisions and from exploitation by the wealthy. Use of the death penalty was rare, even for violent crimes.

Around 2350 BC, Sumeria began to decline in power and importance as vigorous new urban civilizations developed in northern Mesopotamia – ironically, largely due to Sumerian influence. In 2334 BC Sargon, the ruler of the northern city of Agade, conquered a vast swathe of territory from Syria's Mediterranean coast to Sumeria and the Persian Gulf. In doing so, Sargon created a new type of state, the empire, uniting peoples of many different ethnic and cultural identities under his sole rule. Sumeria revived briefly *c.*2100-2000 BC but after that the center of Mesopotamian civilization shifted to the north, to Babylon and Assyria.

CHAPTER THIRTEEN

Civilizations Everywhere

Sumerian civilization did not exist in splendid isolation for long. Elsewhere in the Old World, in the great river valleys of the Lower Nile and the Indus, communities were also developing toward civilization.

Civilization emerged in Egypt after a much shorter period of transition from a simple Neolithic farming way of life than is found in Mesopotamia. The Nile valley was only extensively settled around 4000 BC as farmers were forced out of the eastern Sahara as the climate got drier. Quite suddenly *c*.3100 BC, this simple farming society began to show signs of increasing complexity. Large stone tombs were built with heavy timber roofs which, as Egypt has no timber suitable for building, must have been imported from the Lebanon. Luxury goods made from imported materials like ivory, which could only have been made by specialist craftsmen, were placed in these tombs with the dead. Written records, using the hieroglyphic script, appeared showing that an advanced, centralized administration had been developed. However, Egypt did not see urban growth on the same scale as Sumeria. Towns were smaller and fewer and developed more specialized functions than Sumerian towns, some being exclusively craft centers and others being mainly administrative or religious centers.

Some historians have seen these developments as resulting from Sumerian influence. There was trade between Egypt and Sumeria in the fourth millennium BC and there is some evidence of Sumerian influences on Egyptian art and vocabulary. Hieroglyphic writing is based on the same principle as Sumerian cuneiform (see chapter twelve) but it is otherwise so different that there is no reason to suppose that it was not an indigenous development. Overall, the Sumerian influences seem far too slight to have been a decisive influence.

A more likely cause was rising population

levels in the narrow confines of the Nile valley. Chiefdoms or other forms of centralized authority may have developed by organizing and regulating irrigation works and other farming activities such as marking out field boundaries after the annual Nile flood.

Below: The slate palette of King Narmer, made to commemorate his unification of Egypt *c*.3000 BC. At the top, the king marches toward his decapitated enemies.

The chiefdoms had little room to expand and competition and conflict between them was probably intense. Eventually these chiefdoms amalgamated into two rival kingdoms of Upper (southern) and Lower (northern) Egypt. Finally *c.*3000 BC Narmer (also known as Menes), the ruler of Upper Egypt, conquered Lower Egypt. A finely carved palette, probably carved on Narmer's orders, showing the king standing among the decapitated bodies of his enemies, is the earliest surviving evidence of a united Egyptian kingdom. The subseqent history of the ancient Egyptian kingdom is traditionally divided into five main periods: the Early Dynastic (*c.*3000-2575 BC), the Old Kingdom (*c.*2575-2134 BC), and Middle Kingdom (*c.*2040-1640 BC), the New Kingdom (*c.*1550-1070 BC), and the Late Period (*c.*712-332 BC), interspersed with ''intermediate periods'' of dynastic instability.

Ancient Egyptian civilization depended on the Nile and to a great extent its character was shaped by it. The environment of the Nile valley was much more predictable and dependable than the Mesopotamian plain. Life revolved around the flood which each summer brought water and rich silt from the Ethiopian mountains and East African lakes to almost rainless Egypt. When the floods

Above: Another image of triumphal rulership from Early Dynastic Egypt, the Battlefield Palette shows a lion, symbolizing the king, devouring its enemies, *c.*3000 BC. The appearance of the captives and slain suggests that they were Libyan tribesmen.

receded in the fall, crops were sown. These grew through the warm winter and were harvested in the spring before the next cycle of flooding began. The surpluses were collected as taxes and taken to state storehouses for redistribution to administrators, craftsmen, and priests. With the annual deposition of fresh silt on their fields, Egyptian farmers never faced problems of overcultivation and yields were probably the highest anywhere in the ancient world. The main limitation on productivity was the narrowness of the Nile valley flood plain, only a few hundred yards in places and never wider than a few miles except in the marshy delta. Dykes and canals were built to help divert

governing class taught a doctrine of moderation and fair dealing to all. Greed was the worst sin.

However, the Nile floods could fail, with disastrous consequences, and when this happened it was interpreted as a sign of divine displeasure. The guarantor of the floods was the king (the title pharaoh was not used until 1400 BC). The king was believed to be of divine descent and he was held to be immortal. After his death immense effort was put into the preservation of the king's body by mummification and into providing it with a suitably magnificent tomb. As the king could allow those who served him well to join him in the afterlife, it was worthwhile for all ranks of society to contribute to this effort. At first tombs were built on platforms but these were superseded by pyramids in the reign of King Djoser (2630-2611 BC). The pyramid was the creation of one of Djoser's civil servants, Imhotep, the first architect whose name is known to history. The first pyramids had a stepped construction but by the beginning of the Old Kingdom true pyramids were being built. The greatest of these were built at Giza for the kings Khufu (2551-2528 BC), Khephren (2520-2494 BC), and Menkaure (2490-2472 BC). These great buildings must have strained the resources of the kingdom and later pyramids were more modest affairs. Pyramid building died out at the end of the Middle Kingdom; later Egyptian kings, such as Tutankhamun (1333-1323 BC), were buried in lavishly furnished underground tombs. Contrary to popular belief, the pyramids were not built by slaves (slavery was not as important in ancient Egypt as in most ancient civilizations) but by skilled craftsmen who lived in purpose-built towns and expected to be well rewarded for their work: sometimes they went on strike.

Ancient Egyptian civilization showed remarkable continuity and though Egypt came under foreign rule in the sixth century BC, its culture and way of life continued to flourish for another 900 years, succumbing only to the influence of Christianity c.AD 400. Compared to Egypt, the third of the Old World civilizations to develop, the Indus valley or Harrapan, was a flash in the pan. The Indus civilization emerged c.2500 BC and vanished suddenly and without trace c.1750 BC, it is thought, as a result of an invasion of the Aryan peoples. Civilized life did not re-emerge on the Indian sub-continent for almost a thousand years, by which time all memory of the Indus civilization had been

Left: The first pyramid to be built in Egypt was the step pyramid of King Djoser (2630-2611 BC) at Saqqara. Mortuary temples were attached to these monumental tombs where rites were performed to ensure the eternal well-being of the deceased.

Below left: Terracotta model of a two-wheeled bullock cart similar to those still in use in the Indian sub-continent today: Harrapa, Pakistan, c.3000-2500 BC.

the floodwaters over as wide an area as possible, but even so there were severe limits on how much extra land could be brought into production.

The dependability of the environment gave ancient Egyptian civilization an apparent serenity which is not found in other ancient civilizations: there was enough for everyone. Rarely threatened by invasion before c.1600 BC, for most of its history ancient Egypt was not an overtly militaristic state. The main themes of Egyptian art are religion and country life, while the official statues of the kings watch over the state with calm and benign expressions. The Wisdom Literature which was used to educate the

lost: it was only rediscovered in the 1920s. The Indus is still the most mysterious and least understood of the Old World civilizations because, though literate, its pictographic script has so far proved indecipherable. As a result we know little about the beliefs, customs, social structure, language, or even the ethnic identity of the Indus people: it is thought that they were related to the Dravidian peoples of southern India.

The Indus civilizations probably developed for the same reasons that Sumerian civilization did. The Indus river flood plain has a hot, dry climate similar to Mesopotamia's and agriculture is only possible with irrigation. The Indus floods covered the plain with fertile silt but they were also unpredictable and often destructive. As in Mesopotamia, then, it was probably the need to build and maintain large-scale irrigation works and flood defenses that led to the creation of centralized authorities. There were at least five major cities on the Indus plain and hundreds of lesser settlements. The two largest cities, Mohenjo-daro and Harappa, had populations of around 30-40,000, about four times larger than any of the other cities.

The Indus cities are remarkable for their orderly planning. The cities were laid out on

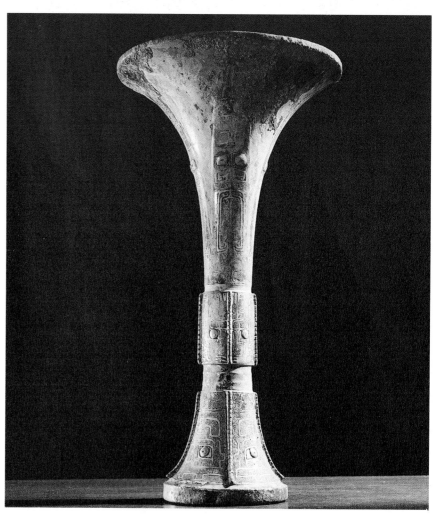

a grid pattern with different areas reserved for different occupations and activities. Brick sewers ran underneath the streets with manholes at intervals to give laborers access for maintenance work. At Mohenjo-daro almost every house had its own bathroom and lavatory connected by drains to the street sewer. The cities were dominated by fortified citadel mounds where, it is presumed, the rulers lived. The citadels contained huge granaries and monumental but unostentatious brick-built public halls where audiences were held.

Above left: Steatite seal with the zebu, the typical Indian cattle, and an inscription, Mohenjo-daro, Pakistan, 2500-2000 BC. The Indus valley civilization's script has not yet been fully deciphered but the few symbols that have been appear to represent words that are related to the modern Dravidian languages of southern India.

Right: Bronze dancing girl, Mohenjo-daro, *c.*2500 BC.

Left: A bronze ritual vessel of the Shang civilization, Tsinan, China, *c.*1500 BC.

The citadels also contained religious buildings. At Mohenjo-daro the center of religious life was a great bathing pool lined with bitumen-sealed brick enclosed within an impressive colonnaded precinct. Bathers entered to perform ritual ablutions by steps at either end of the pool. Although such well-planned towns were clearly the product of a highly organized society, we know nothing at all about the rulers of the Indus civilization. Were they priests, bureaucrats, or kings? There are no lavish burials and little official art from which to judge.

The fourth of the great river valley civilizations of the Old World emerged in the Yellow River valley in China. The roots of Chinese civilization lie in the Longshan period (*c.*5000-2700 BC). By the end of this period, warlike chiefdoms had emerged on the Yangtze plain. Longshan society was marked by sharp economic distinctions between the mass of peasant farmers and craftsmen, and a repressive ruling elite who combined military and spiritual authority. The chiefs lived in small towns defended by rammed earth walls and were given lavish burials accompanied by prestige goods and human sacrifices. Later Chinese historical traditions indicate, credibly, that the first Chinese state emerged as a consequence of conflict between these chiefdoms and the need to organize massive flood defense programs to try to contain the violently unpredictable Yellow River. These traditions place these events in the third millennium BC but there is no archeological evidence for the existence of a civilized state in China before the Shang period (*c.*1750-1100 BC).

The Shang class structure shows continuity with the Longshan period with a small, wealthy aristocracy and a mass of peasant farmers, slaves, and hereditary craftsmen. The king was divine and the royal ancestors were intermediaries between him and the ultimate ancestor of the dynasty, the creator-god Shang Di. Shang kings were buried in great splendor and were accompanied in death by dozens of their slaves and retainers. Around the royal graves were grouped hundreds of lesser burials, most of them containing the decapitated and dismembered bodies of more sacrificial victims. The main source of historical information about the Shang state are the "oracle bones": tortoise shells and animal shoulder blades which were used for divination. On these is found the earliest writing in China, an early version of the ideographic script still used by the Chinese today. Questions addressed by the king to his royal ancestors were written on the bones, which were then cracked. The ancestors' reply was then read from the shape and size of the fissures and often also recorded on the bone. The Shang also kept written administrative records of crop yields and tax returns.

Shang cities boasted formidable fortifications. The Shang capital at Zhengzhou was surrounded by a rammed earth wall 33 feet high and nearly 5 miles long. It is estimated that a workforce of 10,000, laboring for 330 days a year, would have taken 18 years to build the walls. Only members of the elite were allowed to live within the walled compound, craftsmen and laborers lived in their own settlements outside. Shang craftsmen worked to high standards in bone, lacquer, jade, pottery, silk, and wool. However, the real artistic and technological triumph of the Shang was in bronze casting. Instead of the lost-wax method of bronze casting used elsewhere in Eurasia at this time, the Shang used a sophisticated piece-mold technique to cast shapes of great intricacy.

Around 1100 BC the Shang were overthrown by a nomadic people from the west who founded the Chou dynasty (c.1100-211 BC). Like many later invaders of China, the Chou were quickly absorbed by the Chinese and there was no break in cultural development. Under the Chou, civilization began to spread throughout China, but the power of the kings declined and the Chou kingdom eventually broke up into a host of warring states. In 221 BC, Shi Huangdi, ruler of the Qin state, conquered the other Chinese states and established the empire which theoretically came to an end with the deposition of the last emperor in 1911 but which in reality still survives as the People's Republic of China. If the success of a civilization is to be measured solely by its longevity, then Chinese civilization, with over 3500 years of cultural continuity, has a good claim to be the world's most successful.

The other contender for the title of "world's most successful civilization" has to be the European because of the enormous global influence it has achieved. The first European civilization developed on the Aegean island of Crete c.2000 BC. Unlike the civilizations of Egypt, Sumeria, the Indus, and China, the Minoan civilization (named after Minos, a mythological king of Crete) did not develop on an alluvial flood plain, nor did it depend on irrigation. The basis of Minoan subsistence was the "Mediterranean Triad" of wheat, vines, and olives. These

Left: Shang bronze vessels, libation jug (*above*), and a sacrificial food vessel (*below*), both twelfth century BC. The four legs of the sacrificial food vessel symbolize power, upright government, and the stability of the state – remove one leg and the vessel topples.

Above: Reconstruction of part of the Minoan palace at Knossos, Crete, *c.*1450 BC. Minoan palaces were centers for the collection and redistribution of countryside produce and trade goods.

provided the Minoans with a balanced diet and two valuable commodities, wine and olive oil, which were traded widely in the eastern Mediterranean. Through this trade the Minoans had contacts with Egypt and the Near East, but civilization in Crete developed entirely independently of outside influences as a result of the island's prosperity.

The focuses of Minoan civilization were the palaces of Knossos, Phaestos, Mallia, and Zakro. These palaces were built on a massive scale and functioned almost as small towns, being the homes of the rulers of Crete as well as administrative and economic centers. The palaces housed archives, workshops for craftsmen, shrines, audience chambers, and storerooms where food surpluses and trade goods were concentrated for redistribution. The needs of administra-

tion led to the development of writing, first using a hieroglyphic system and later using a script known as Linear A. Neither has been deciphered. Minoan civilization was evidently peaceful, for the palaces were unfortified. Around 1450 BC Minoan civilization suffered a shattering setback as a result of earthquakes and ash falls following a massive volcanic eruption on the Aegean island of Thera. Crete was subsequently conquered by the Mycenaean people of the Greek mainland. The Mycenaeans introduced a form of the Minoan script known as Linear B and other Minoan practices to the mainland. Linear B was brilliantly deciphered in 1952 by Michael Ventris, who had worked as a code-breaker during World War II, and was found to record an early form of the Greek language.

The Mycenaean civilization was much more warlike than the Minoan and its settlements, like Mycenae, were often heavily fortified. The Mycenaean aristocracy were buried with hoards of weapons, war became a major subject of art and inventories of weapons are found on clay tablets. Around 1200 BC, Mycenaean civilization collapsed, probably as a result of outside invasion. Greece entered a "dark age" from which it only began to recover 400 years later, by which time the Minoans and Mycenaeans were remembered only dimly in Greek mythology. The brilliant civilization of classical Greece owed more to the Near East than to Crete and represents the true beginning of European civilization.

The Americas saw the development of primary civilizations in Mesoamerica and Peru. The first Mesoamerican civilization was the Olmec, which flourished in the tropical rainforests of the Bay of Campeche c.1200 BC-c.AD 1. Tropical rainforests are not generally favorable to the development of civilizations. Tropical forest soils are of very poor quality and are exhausted after only two to three years of cultivation. Consequently the normal pattern of rainforest

Left: A crude but effective suit of Mycenaean bronze armor, c.1400-1200 BC. The helmet made of boar's teeth was a distinctive feature of a Mycenaean warrior's equipment.

Below left: Large clay storage jar from the Minoan palace at Knossos, 1450-1400 BC. The palace storerooms contained hundreds of such jars which were used for storing grain, wine, and olive oil until they were issued as rations to the palace staff.

Right: The monumental Lion Gate at Mycenae, Greece, built c.1250 BC. Mycenae's defensive walls were built of stone blocks so massive that later Greeks believed they could only have been built by giants.

farming is the shifting "slash and burn" method. This precludes the growth of large concentrations of population – one of the prerequisites for the development of civilizations.

When civilizations do develop in rainforests, we must look for special factors. In the case of the Olmec, the special factor was the presence of fertile river flood plains which could support large populations without losing their fertility. Year round warmth and water supply made it possible for the Olmec to raise four crops of maize a year. Not all farmers had equal access to the best land on the flood plains and this led to the growth of class divisions and the emergence of a hierarchical society governed by powerful hereditary chiefs. The chiefs ruled from ceremonial centers which were the nearest thing the Olmec had to towns. These contained earth "pyramids" and impressive monumental stone sculptures of warrior chiefs and gods. The populations of these centers were small, one of the largest, San Lorenzo, had only about 2500 inhabitants. Trade or gift exchange played an important part in Olmec civilization as obsidian for toolmaking and jade and basalt for carving all had to be imported. The Olmec developed a system of writing based on hieroglyphs

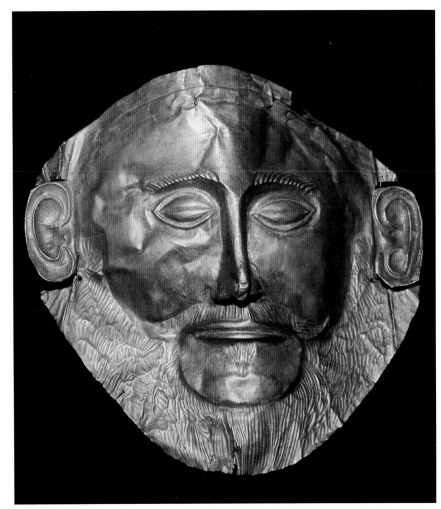

Above: Gold death mask of a Mycenaean king, *c.*1550 BC.

Left: The massive carved basalt head of an Olmec warrior chief, San Lorenzo, Mexico, 1200-900 BC. The stone for the 6-feet tall sculpture had to be imported from mountains 50 miles to the west.

Right: Clay figure of a Maya scribe writing, Jaina Island, Mexico, *c.* AD 800. The Olmec developed a simple hieroglyphic script which was developed into a complete writing system by the Maya.

Far right: Mayan temple pyramid at Tikal, Guatemala, eighth century AD. Mesoamerican pyramids are similar in conception to the Mesopotamian ziggurats in that they were essentially elevated platforms for temples.

which has been only partially deciphered. Many inscriptions are calendrical in content and it seems that the Olmec invented the 260-day year and the 52-year "long-count" calendar, both of which came to be widely used in Mesoamerica. Though Olmec civilization disappeared in the first century AD, its cultural influence was reflected in the Zapotec civilization of the Oaxaca valley and the Maya civilization of the Yucatán which succeeded it and built on its achievements.

The last of the world's primary civilizations developed in the Peruvian Andes. Here complex societies emerged as a means of organizing intensified agricultural exploitation in an environmentally diverse region. The transition from coastal lowland to high mountain in Peru is abrupt. Lowland agriculture was based on maize, beans, and squash, while in the highlands root crops like potatoes predominated. By maintaining colonies in both highland and lowland zones, communities could greatly increase the diversity of resources available to them, but strong leadership was needed to co-ordinate the colonies' activities and to keep the communities united. Irrigation in the lowlands and terracing in the highlands could also be used to intensify production, with a consequent need for a centralized organizing body. Complex chiefdoms, represented by the Chavin and Páracas cultures, had begun to develop in both coastal and mountain areas of Peru by 1000 BC. By 200 BC the Moche and Nazca cultures were showing signs of considerable social stratification and craft specialization, but it was not until c.AD 600 that regional states began to emerge. The most important of these was Tiahuanaco, a sprawling city with remarkable megalithic architecture on an island in Lake Titicaca. Tiahuanaco was followed by a succession of Andean states, culminating in the establishment of the vast Inca Empire in 1438.

The civilizations of Peru show the wisdom of seeking to define "civilization" primarily in terms of social organization. None of the Andean states was literate, on which grounds some historians refuse to recognize them as true civilizations, and their technology was simple yet they were undeniably highly organized and sophisticated societies. The hierarchical administrative structure of the Inca Empire was a particularly impressive achievement. The empire was divided into four quarters which were ruled by the emperor from the capital Cuzco. Below the emperor were the prefects of the four quarters and below them, provincial governors, district officers, and, at the bottom, foremen responsible for 50-100 families each. Taxes were paid as labor service on state farms, public building and irrigation projects, and military service. Tax and census records were kept on "quipus," complex mnemonic devices made of knotted strings. Different colored strings were used on a quipu to symbolize different items or services, while the number of knots indicated the quantities held or required. A 12,000-mile long system of roads and way stations, second only to that of the Roman Empire among ancient civilizations, was built to improve internal communications and Quechua, the Inca language, was successfully imposed throughout the empire. The further development of Inca civilization was abruptly cut off by the Spanish conquest of 1532.

The most striking feature of the American civilizations is their lack of technological accomplishments, not least their failure to adopt the wheel. This is particularly strange because the principle of the wheel was known in the Americas but was not applied to anything other than children's toys. The

Right: One of the greatest achievements of the Andean civilizations were their superb quality textiles, made usually on the simple back-strap loom: seen here still in use by modern Andean weavers. Textiles were an important source of wealth and a major item of exchange between rulers. Textiles were used as sacrificial offerings to the gods, to mark important moments in life and to wrap the dead.

Below: The Inca fort of Sacsahuaman, near Cuzco, Peru, c. AD 1450. The massive stones of the walls were meticulously shaped to fit one another exactly. If a stone was found not to fit exactly when it was moved into place it was simply removed and reshaped, even it weighed several tons.

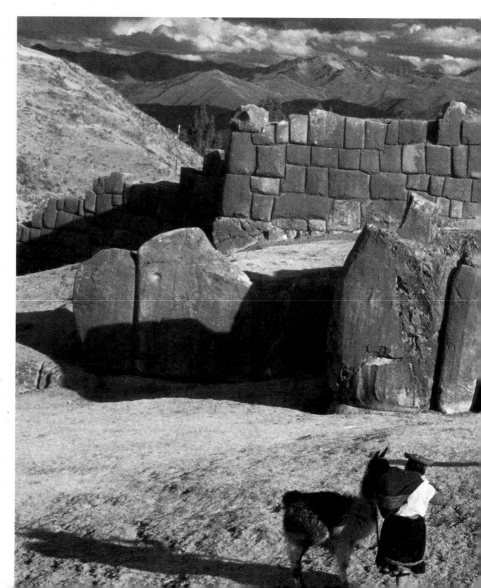

lack of suitable draught animals is the usual explanation given for this but, while this would have limited the wheel's usefulness, it does not seem to be an entirely satisfactory answer. Why, for example, was the wheel never used to make pottery? Whatever the reason, it serves as a useful reminder that a sophisticated technology is not a prerequisite of civilized life.

The emergence of civilizations around the world marks the end of the history of early man. When we look at an early city like Uruk or Mohenjo-daro, we can see that their populations lived a way of life which is recognizably akin to our own – hierarchical, literate, specialized, regulated, policed, and taxed – and far more complex than that of any earlier society. The ancient civilizations established a pattern of social and economic life which, despite enormous differences of scale, ideology, and technological accomplishment, continued to be the primary characteristic of all subsequent civilizations until as little as 250 years ago. The achievements of pre-industrial civilizations were based primarily on the organized muscle power of men and animals. The success of a civilization depended entirely on the productivity of the agricultural labor force and the efficiency of the state in controlling and redistributing its food surpluses. The mass of people continued to live simple lives working the land and surrendering much of their produce to support an elite which, alone, enjoyed the fruits of civilization. If for

any reason, such as war, depopulation, or soil exhaustion, agricultural productivity collapsed, the civilization was also likely to collapse. This fate befell the Sumerians, the Romans, the Maya, and many others. The close relationship between agriculture and civilization only began to change in the eighteenth century when the Industrial Revolution led to manufacturing becoming the principal source of wealth.

Above: Nazca pot, Peru, *c.*AD 1-700. Nazca potters were highly skilled at producing richly decorated polychrome vessels.

Below: Locations of early civilizations.

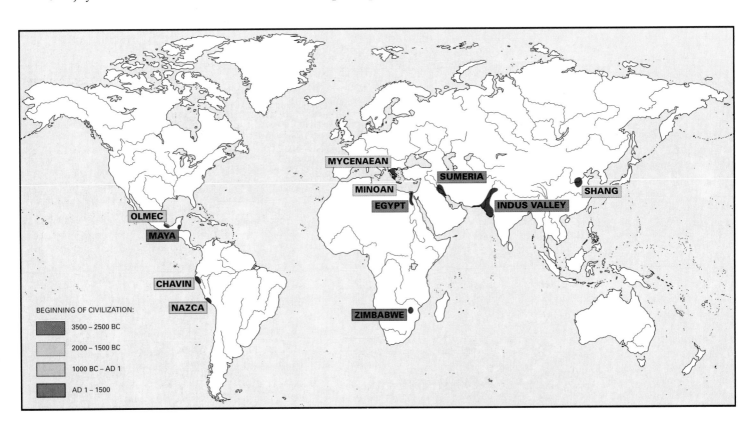

BEGINNING OF CIVILIZATION:

3500 – 2500 BC

2000 – 1500 BC

1000 BC – AD 1

AD 1 – 1500

OLMEC

MAYA

CHAVIN

NAZCA

MYCENAEAN

MINOAN

EGYPT

SUMERIA

INDUS VALLEY

SHANG

ZIMBABWE

Select Bibliography

General

Clarke, G., *The Identity of Man* (Methuen, London, 1983).
Fagan, B. M., *People of the Earth* (Harper Collins, New York, 7th edn, 1992).
Hayden, B., *Archaeology: the Science of Once and Future Things* (Freeman, New York, 1993).
Renfrew, C. & Bahn, P., *Archaeology: Theories, Methods and Practice* (Thames and Hudson, London, 1991).

Human Evolution and Paleolithic Man

Bahn, P. & Vertut, J., *Images of the Ice Age* (Facts on File, 1989).
Fagan, B. M., *The Journey from Eden: the Peopling of Our World* (Thames and Hudson, 1990).
Gamble, C., *Timewalkers: the Prehistory of Global Colonization* (Alan Sutton, 1993).
Johanson, D. & Shreeve, J. *Lucy's Child* (William Morrow, 1989).
Leakey, R., *The Origin of Humankind* (Weidenfeld, 1994).
Nelson, H. & Jurmain, R., *Introduction to Physical Anthropology* (West, St Paul, 5th edn, 1991).
Schick, K. D. & Toth, N., *Making Silent Stones Speak: Human Evolution and the Dawn of Technology* (Simon and Schuster, New York, 1993).
Stringer, C. & Gamble, C., *In Search of the Neanderthals* (Thames and Hudson, 1993).
Wills, C., *The Runaway Brain: the Evolution of Human Uniqueness* (Basic Books, 1993).

Studies of Regional Prehistory

Clark, J. D., *The Prehistory of Africa* (Thames and Hudson, London, 1970).
Cunliffe, B. (ed.), *The Oxford Illustrated Prehistory of Europe* (Oxford University Press, 1994).
Darvill, T., *Prehistoric Britain* (Batsford, London, 1987).
Fagan, B. M., *Ancient North America* (Thames and Hudson, 1991).
Fiedel, S. J., *Prehistory of the Americas* (Cambridge University Press, 2nd edn, 1992).
Flood, J., *Archaeology of the Dreamtime* (Hawaii UP, 1988).
Jensen, J., *The Prehistory of Denmark* (London, 1982).

Hunter-Gatherers

Coon, C., *The Hunting Peoples* (London, 1987).
Drucker, P., *Indians of the North-West Coast* (New York, 1963).
Dummond, D., *The Eskimos and Aleuts* (Thames and Hudson, 1977).
Lee, R. B., *The !Kung San* (Cambridge University Press, 1979).
Service, E. R., *The Hunters* (Prentice Hall, Englewood Cliffs N.J., 1966).
Smith, C., *Late Stone Age Hunters of the British Isles* (Routledge, London-New York, 1992).

Early Farmers

Childe, V. G., *Man Makes Himself* (London, 1936).
Hedges, J. W., *Tomb of the Eagles: a Window on Stone Age Tribal Britain* (John Murray, London, 1984).
Renfrew, C., *Before History* (Knopf, New York, 1973).
Richards, J. D., *Stonehenge* (Batsford, London, 1991).
Rindos, D., *The Origins of Agriculture* (Academic Press, New York, 1984).
Sahlins, M., *Tribesmen* (Prentice Hall, Englewood Cliffs N.J., 1968).

The First Civilizations

Aldred, C., *The Egyptians* (Thames and Hudson, London, revised edn, 1984).
Banks, G., *Peru before Pizarro* (Phaidon, Oxford, 1977).
Chang, K. C., *The Archaeology of Ancient China* (Yale UP, 1977).
Crawford, H., *Sumer and the Sumerians* (Cambridge University Press, 1991).
Hood, S., *The Minoans* (Thames and Hudson, London, 1973).
Kemp, B., *Ancient Egypt* (Routledge London-New York, 1989).
Redman, C. L., *The Rise of Civilization: from Early Farmers to Urban Society in the Ancient Near East* (Freeman, San Francisco, 1978).
Roaf, M., *Cultural Atlas of Mesopotamia and the Ancient Near East* (Facts on File, New York, 1990).
Soustelle, J., *The Olmecs: the Oldest Civilization in Mexico* (New York, 1984).
Taylour, Lord W., *The Mycenaeans* (Thames and Hudson, London, 2nd edn, 1990).
Wheeler, M., *The Indus Civilization* (Cambridge University Press, 1968).
Whitehouse, R. & Wilkins, J., *The Making of Civilization* (Knopf, New York, 1988).

Index

Acknowledgments

The publisher would like to thank David Eldred for designing this book, Caroline Earle for editing it, Suzanne O'Farrell and Rita Longabucco for the picture research, Simon Shelmerdine for production, and Ron Watson for compiling the index. Thanks also to Richard Natkiel for drawing the maps and Graham Bingham for the diagrams. The following individuals and agencies provided photographic material:
Heather Angel: pages 10, 16.
Association Louis Bégouën/ Robert Bégouën: page 78(bottom).
The Bettmann Archive: pages 26, 33(bottom), 37, 79, 101(top), 140(top), 142.
Biofotos/Guy Yeoman: page 17.
The British Museum, London: pages 27(bottom right), 50, 103.
Bruce Coleman Ltd/Peter Davey: pages 2-3, 18.
C. M. Dixon Photo Resources: pages 1, 6, 7(top right, bottom left, and center), 9 (top right), 12(both), 14, 15(bottom), 24(center), 29(top), 32(bottom), 34, 35, 36(bottom), 39, 42, 45(both), 46, 47, 48(both), 49, 52, 53, 58-59, 62(both), 66, 70(bottom), 73, 74-75(both), 80, 81(bottom), 88, 94, 95(top), 97, 102(bottom), 105, 107, 108, 111(top), 113(both), 114(top, center, and bottom left), 116, 117(bottom), 118, 122(top), 123, 130, 132, 133, 135, 136(both), 137(both), 138, 139(top), 141, 143, 144(both), 146(top), 148(top), 149, 150(both), 151, 153(top and bottom left), 156(top).
Collection Privé Dr. Robert Donceel: pages 117(top), 120(top).
Robert Estall Photographs/ David Coulson: pages 82, 83.
ffotograff/Charles Aithie: pages 57, 65, 86-87(bottom); **/Patricia Aithie:** pages 109, 111(bottom), 119(bottom), 120(bottom), 128.
Werner Forman Archive: pages 20(right), 100, 146(bottom), 148(bottom), 152.
Sonia Halliday Photographs: pages 104, 115(bottom right), 121.
John Haywood: pages 110, 122(bottom), 125.
Hirmer Fotoarchiv: page 134.
Hulton Deutsch Collection Ltd: pages 7(top left), 38, 40; **/Gould:** page 21(right).
Irish Tourist Board: pages 126-127.

Life File/Sue Davies: page 129;/ **Abbie Enock:** pages 84, 86(top), 89, 91(both), 119(top);/ **Tim Fisher:** page 71;/**David Heath:** pages 85, 93(top left, bottom);/**Juliet Highet:** pages 81(top), 154-155(bottom);/**Hugh Pond:** page 44;/**Richard Powers:** page 153(bottom right);/**Nigel Sitwell:** page 124;/ **Andy Teare:** page 11;/**Flora Torrance:** page 55(bottom);/ **Andrew Ward:** page 93(top right);/**Eric Wilkins:** page 95(center).
Lowie Museum of Anthropology, University of California: pages 98-99.
The Mansell Collection: pages 14, 139(bottom), 147.
Collection Photothèque du Musée de l'Homme, Paris: page 30(bottom).
National Archives, U.S.A.: pages 54-55(top).
National Museum of Copenhagen: page 102(top).
National Museum of Prehistory, Dordogne, France: pages 67, 70(top).
National Museums of Kenya: pages 25(top), 29(bottom), 30(top).
Natural History Museum, London: pages 21(left), 27(top left), 32(top), 36(top), 41.

N. E. Stock Photo/Jim Schwabel: pages 60;/**Clyde H. Smith:** page 63.
Novosti: page 72.
Photo Network: page 19;/ **Nancy Hoyt Belcher:** page 61;/**W. M. Mitchell:** page 155(top);/**Mark Sherman:** page 24(top);/**Paul Thompson:** pages 4-5.
La Réunion des Musées Nationaux, Paris: pages 31(top), 51, 68, 69, 76-77, 78(top), 95(bottom), 101(bottom);/**G. Blot:** pages 106, 112.
Reuters/Bettmann: pages 114-115(bottom center).
Smithsonian Institution: pages 56, 64;/**National Museum of the American Indian:** page 96.
Ulster History Park: page 92.
University of the Witwatersrand, Johannesburg/R. J. Clarke: page 24(bottom);/**Alun Hughes:** page 22(both).
UPI/Bettmann: pages 8(top left), 20(left), 25(bottom), 33(top).
John Wymer: page 43.
Zoological Society of London: page 15(top).